12 Session Workbook

INCREASE
Unleash God's Direction For Your Finances

ZACH SANTMIER

Scripture quotations taken from the (NASB®) New American Standard Bible®, Copyright © 1960, 1971, 1977, 1995, 2020 by The Lockman Foundation. Used by permission. All rights reserved. lockman.org

All quotations in call out bubbles are taken from the Author, Zach Santmier.

The content of this workbook along with its associated video curriculum is protected by U.S. and International laws. Reproduction and distribution of this material without written permission of the sponsor is prohibited.

© 2023 by Zach Santmier

Table of Contents

Meet the Team
   Zach Bio
   Andrew Bio

01. What is Biblical Stewardship?

02. Roadblocks to Biblical Stewardship

03. Finding Your Purpose

04. Roadblocks to Finding Your Purpose

05. The Necessity of a Sustainable Financial System

06. Increase Your Income

07. 1/8th – Balanced Budget

08. 2/8 – Give 10%, 3/8 – New Zero in Checking, 4/8 – Adequate Insurance

09. 5/8 – Consumer Debt

10. 6/8 – Invest 15%, 7/8 – New Zero in Savings, 8/8 – Housing at 25%

11. Build Your Legacy

12. Ready, Set, Increase!

Resources

THE
INCREASE
MOVEMENT

MEET THE AUTHOR

Zach Santmier is passionate about seeing the world INCREASE all God has given them. His passion started shortly after graduating from Cedarville University and getting a job as a Worship Pastor. As a pastor's kid, working in the Church was something Zach had always envisioned. However, thanks to a mentor and friend, he realized that shortly after starting a career in ministry, he was being called into the business world. In a dramatic turn of events, opposed to moving to Boston to go to seminary, Zach moved from Ohio to Michigan with his wife who was pregnant with their oldest daughter. Zach's move changed his trajectory, and instead of working at a church, he found himself full time in the business world.

For the past decade, Zach has been building and growing Trumble Insurance Agency, a third generation family business. Since 2015, he has been an owner and took over full ownership in 2020. He has led his team of insurance professionals to earn more 5-star Google reviews than any other agency in the state of Michigan, a statistic that demonstrates their effort in creating a best in class customer experience. In 2020, Zach helped launch Inheritance Church where he still serves on the board and as a Teaching Pastor.

Zach simultaneously owns Trumble Agency while serving as a Teaching Pastor. His combined experiences give him a unique perspective into stewardship in the Kingdom of God. This project, The Increase Movement, is the culmination of the lessons he has learned, principles he has studied, and the call of God on His life to serve the Church.

Personally, Zach is a girl dad to three beautiful princesses. His wife, Lauren, homeschools their girls and together, Zach and Lauren love taking their kiddos on hikes and spending as much time outside as possible. Though he likes golf, hunting and fishing, he has realized that those will be enjoyed later in life when "free time" becomes a thing again.

Zach Santmier

INCREASE

THE
INCREASE
MOVEMENT

MEET YOUR HOST

Andrew Wingeier is the Chief Operating Officer of The Increase Movement. For the past decade, he has held executive-level roles as a CFO and Executive Director of Finance & Operations within the non-profit sector. In a previous role as CFO for a large, rapidly expanding congregation that averaged 5,000 attendees each weekend, Andrew was entrusted with the stewardship of a $12 million budget. His leadership role on the Executive Team overseeing 87 staff members offered him a unique vantage point, allowing him to collaborate with other large churches and church-related organizations across the nation, fostering invaluable networks and insights.

His passion is deeply rooted in fostering operational efficiency and championing missions that resonate with his values. This passion has led him to collaborate with Zach as they bring this message of biblical stewardship to the world.

Andrew is married to his high school sweetheart, Ryann. Together, they have two beautiful daughters. He loves golf, following sports, and a good spreadsheet!

Andrew Wingeier

INCREASE

INCREASE

1

Session 1
What Is Biblical Stewardship?

Christians have defined stewardship as "appropriately allocating resources." Out of fear of being prideful, Christians have hidden their talents in the backyard and protected what they have been given. As the parable of the talents shows us, this is the opposite of what stewardship in the Kingdom of God looks like. Christians are called to steward their talents and treasures towards increase! It is time for christians to be the light of the world, not a light hidden and protected under a bushel.

Stewardship in the Kingdom of God

Session 1
What is Biblical Stewardship?

Introduction

> "In Italy, the Church was the cultural influence around the time of the Renaissance. Art, science, and morality came from the Church."

_____

Once the church gained _____ and _____, leaders switched from _____ towards _____.

_____
_____
_____
_____

Christians have focused on not _____ what they have instead of _____ what they have been given.

_____
_____
_____
_____

Answer key

influence
prominence
growing
protecting
losing
increasing
water
seed
blossom
increase

It's time to _____ the _____ God has placed in each of our lives and begin seeing God's plans and purposes _____ into maturity as we steward towards _____!

_____
_____
_____
_____

Stewardship in the Kingdom of God

> **Session 1**
> What is Biblical Stewardship?

Breakout Questions

1. What was your drive like when you first started working? Do you remember any examples where you did something to grow, learn, or make more money?

2. Have you ever seen someone else change from that youthful excitement of growth towards protecting? What did you learn as you watched their shift?

Part 1
Stewardship Requires Increase

"The word of God is _____ and _____ and sharper than any _____."
- Hebrews 4:12

Answer key
living
active
two-edged sword

Stewardship in the Kingdom of God

Session 1
What is Biblical Stewardship?

The Parable of the Talents shows us the
_____ _____.

_____
_____
_____
_____

All He asks is that we operate, not out of _____, but out of _____ , knowing that He is a good master and that in Him, we have all we need to grow the seed He has sown in our lives.

_____
_____
_____
_____

The fear of God that leads us to _____ is exactly what the _____ is speaking against.

_____
_____
_____
_____

Answer key

- Father's heart
- fear
- relationship
- inaction
- Parable of the Talents

Stewardship in the Kingdom of God

> **Session 1**
> What is Biblical Stewardship?

Breakout Questions

1. What fears lead to not seeking increase and multiplication in the resources God has given us?

2. How have you seen others bury what they've been given? What talents, dreams, finances, or opportunities have you seen in people's backyards?

Part 2
Money and Purpose – Fuel and Directions

We all _____ knowing our _____ or our _____.

🔒 **Answer key**

crave
purpose
calling in life

Stewardship in the Kingdom of God

Session 1
What is Biblical Stewardship?

We search for _____ and without it, we use phrases like "we feel lost." That "lost" feeling is because we lack the _____ that _____ provides.

_____
_____
_____
_____

Answer key

feeling
calling
purpose
direction
meaning

Your _____ is worth _____.

_____
_____
_____
_____

Breakout Questions

1. Can you remember a dream that you once had that you gave up on or justified out of existence? What was it and why did you stop going after it?

Stewardship in the Kingdom of God

Session 1
What is Biblical Stewardship?

2. What do you believe is the purpose of money? Up until now, how have you viewed your bank accounts?

Most people never stick to financial plans and systems because they are not _____ to their core _____ here on earth.

When we view our money as the _____ to be who God created us to be, we become more _____ and _____ connected to stewarding our finances.

Answer key

spiritually
emotionally
fuel
purposes
connected

Stewardship in the Kingdom of God

> **Session 1**
> What is Biblical Stewardship?

Breakout Questions

1. What has been your experience with other financial courses and have you been able to stick to them? Why or why not?

2. Discuss Zach's definition of money: fuel for the journey. How does that definition change the way you view your personal finances?

Session 1 Homework

Did you learn any new perspectives from what you heard in this first session? Did anything not sit well with you that you may not agree with or have more questions about? Write down your thoughts, and as this course goes on, look for answers to these questions or concerns.

Session 1
What is Biblical Stewardship?

Stewardship in the Kingdom of God

Personal Reflection: Reflect on your own journey of faith and stewardship. How do you currently view the role of the Church and individual Christians in society?

Scripture Reflection: Read Matthew 25:14-30, the Parable of the Talents. Reflect on how this passage speaks to the concept of stewardship in your life and note any new insights or questions that arise.

INCREASE

2

Session 2
Roadblocks to Biblical Stewardship

To pursue money and wealth is fleeting and futile. This partial truth has led many people to not pursue wealth and success. However, if we appropriately understand our endgame of becoming who God created us to be, we will be able to view money in its rightful position: fuel for the journey. To love money and pursue financial targets that are independent of purpose targets is evil and meaningless. Money in and of itself doesn't provide meaning or purpose, but financial success should and must be pursued as we steward what God has given us to increase.

Stewardship in the Kingdom of God

Session 2
Roadblocks to Biblical Stewardship

Reflection from Last Session

Share your observations from Matthew 25:14-30 & Acts 18:1-4 that we discussed last week. Feel free to flip back to your Session 1 homework to refresh your memory!

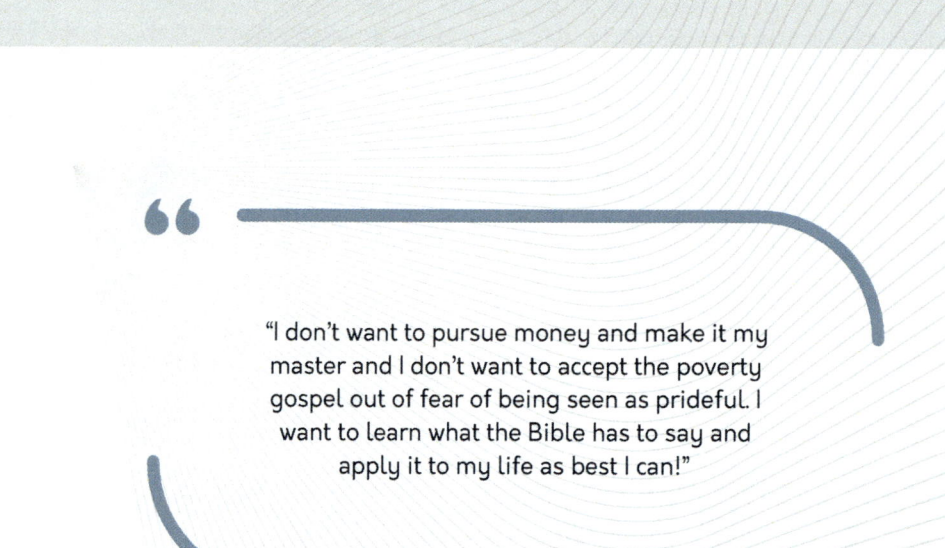

> "I don't want to pursue money and make it my master and I don't want to accept the poverty gospel out of fear of being seen as prideful. I want to learn what the Bible has to say and apply it to my life as best I can!"

Truly understanding a verse requires examining its complete context. Overcoming narrow interpretations of single verses is crucial to fully grasp God's intentions and avoid settling for less.

Stewardship in the Kingdom of God

Session 2
Roadblocks to Biblical Stewardship

Roadblock 1
The Love of Money is the Root of All Evil

"9 But those who want to get rich fall into temptation and a snare and many foolish and harmful desires which plunge men into ruin and destruction. 10 For the love of money is a root of all sorts of evil, and some by longing for it have wandered away from the faith and pierced themselves with many griefs."

1 Timothy 6:9-10

Timothy is speaking to those who want to get _____ in verse 9. This goes beyond just loving money. This speaks to the _____ or _____ that one is going after.

_____
_____
_____
_____

The _____ of our _____ is never going to be money. As we learned last week, money is _____! Money has a purpose. It's to _____ God's _____ in your life.

_____
_____
_____
_____

Answer key

(inverted):
- purposes
- fuel
- fuel for the journey
- ambition
- target
- target
- goal
- rich

Session 02 // 12 .   Page 21

Stewardship in the Kingdom of God

> **Session 2**
> Roadblocks to Biblical Stewardship

Roadblock 1

In the Kingdom of God, money and wealth should _____ be the pursuit. The _____ of God in our lives are what are meant to be pursued.

Answer key

never
purposes

> "We must continue to view money in its rightful place. Not the destination or the goal, but the fuel for the purposes of God in our lives."

Breakout Questions

1. What sorts of temptation could someone fall into if they increased in wealth quickly?

2. How does it make a difference in our lives when we see God's purpose as our pursuit and money as our fuel?

Stewardship in the Kingdom of God

Session 2
Roadblocks to Biblical Stewardship

Roadblock 2
He must increase and I must... decrease?

"He must increase, but I must decrease." — John 3:30

John's ministry of _____ the path had been _____. He had done what he was called to do, and now was his time to hand the baton to the Messiah.

_____
_____
_____
_____

John wasn't saying that His ministry wasn't _____ or that he was _____.

_____
_____
_____
_____

Answer key
preparing
completed
important
insignificant

"The God who created the heavens and earth doesn't need us to get smaller so that He can get bigger."

Stewardship in the Kingdom of God

Session 2
Roadblocks to Biblical Stewardship

Roadblock 2
He must increase and I must... decrease?

John the Baptist wasn't saying that he needed to decrease his ministry so that Jesus' ministry could look bigger! He was simply saying that it was time for his _____ to come to _____ and Jesus' ministry to _____.

_____
_____
_____
_____

Growing, building, striving for the upward call of Christ should be _____ in the Church. Yes, it must be done in humility, but we should never, out of fear of being seen as proud, _____ growth. And growth in and of itself is not prideful, as the laws of Scandinavia suggest. Growth is _____ and _____ for obedient Christians.

_____
_____
_____
_____

Answer key

ministry
fulfillment
begin
applauded
neglect
biblical
necessary

Stewardship in the Kingdom of God

> **Session 2**
> What is Biblical Stewardship?

Breakout Questions

1. What ways have you seen Christians hide their gifts or be afraid to step out and use what God has given them? What has the world lost because of their fear?

2. How have you experienced the Tall Poppy Syndrome in the Church, either first or second hand? How did this get in the way of God's plan to bring increase through your life or the life of someone you know?

Stewardship in the Kingdom of God

Session 2
Roadblocks to Biblical Stewardship

Roadblock 3
I've learned to be content... and I must increase.

It is absolutely possible to be _____ and also _____ and _____ of _____.

_____
_____
_____
_____

It is necessary to first be _____ before God will bless the work of your hands with _____ and _____ increase.

_____
_____
_____
_____

_____ is not being _____ with where you are at, but resting in _____ you are _____.

_____
_____
_____
_____

Answer key

content
pursue
dream
more
content
meaningful
lasting
Contentment
complacent
Who
with

Session 02 // 12.   Page 26

Stewardship in the Kingdom of God

Session 2
Roadblocks to Biblical Stewardship

Roadblock 3
I've learned to be content... and I must increase.

_____ often comes from feeling that _____ you are doesn't allow you to be, do, or have what you _____.

_____
_____
_____
_____

Contentment is realizing that God has _____ you to be everything God has _____ you to be. Nothing more and nothing less.

_____
_____
_____
_____

Answer key

Discontentment
where
want
empowered
called
anything
everything
called

When we are content, we realize that we can do _____ he has called us to do. And we can be _____ He has _____ us to be.

_____
_____
_____
_____

Stewardship in the Kingdom of God

Session 2
What is Biblical Stewardship?

Breakout Questions

1. What areas of life do you find yourself being discontent? What causes you to feel discontent in those moments?

Session 2 Homework

1. Name your top three roadblocks that have stopped you from pursuing God's fullness for your life? Why have they stopped you? Were there words spoken against you? Did you grow up with a distorted view of God or even of yourself?

2. Read through Ephesians 2:10 this week. Meditate on this passage as we prepare our hearts for the next session. What is God saying to you through this passage? Spend time meditating and praying through this verse several times this week.

INCREASE

3

Session 3
Finding Your Purpose

Ephesians 2 says that God has prepared good works for all of His children to walk in. The question we must ask ourselves and God is, "What are those good works for me?" There are three levels of purpose or calling that we see throughout Scripture. There is a general purpose, a personal purpose, and a specific purpose.

General   Personal   Specific

G   P   S

Stewardship in the Kingdom of God

Session 3
Finding Your Purpose

> **Session 3**
> Finding Your Purpose

Money is ____ for the _____!

_____
_____
_____
_____

Zach's Sermon on Ephesians 3

Answer key

fuel
journey

> "Don't you want to know where you're going? Don't you want to have a clear path to walk down that isn't full of unknowns, trials and errors, last minute directions, starts and stops? I know I do. You can have all of the money in the world, or fuel for the journey, but if you don't know where you're headed, it will be useless."

Stewardship in the Kingdom of God

Session 3
Finding Your Purpose

> **Session 3**
> Finding Your Purpose

Your _ _ _ _ _ and _ _ _ _ _ _ _ are _ _ _ _ _ _ _ _ _ _ _ _.

_____
_____
_____
_____

Paul, before his calling was confirmed by the leaders of the early church, spent _ _ _ _ _ _ _ _ _ _ _ stewarding his call towards increase.

_____
_____
_____
_____

Answer key

money
purpose
connected
17 years
inaction
powerful

Paul certainly had a lot of questions, but those questions didn't lead him to _ _ _ _ _ _ _ _. He took one step forward at a time and in so doing, walked into one of the most _ _ _ _ _ _ _ _ _ _ callings of all times outside of Jesus.

_____
_____
_____
_____

Stewardship in the Kingdom of God

Session 3
Finding Your Purpose

> ## Session 3
> Finding Your Purpose

You have a _____ Purpose, a _____ Purpose, and a _____ Purpose. _____

_____
_____
_____
_____

If you use this _____, you will begin to see God's plans _____, not _____.

_____
_____
_____
_____

God has given us _____ we need pertaining to _____ and _____.

_____
_____
_____
_____

Answer key

General
Personal
Specific
G.P.S.
G.P.S.
unfold
unveil
everything
life
godliness

> Ephesians 2:10 "For we are God's handiwork, created in Christ Jesus to do good works, which God prepared in advance for us to do."

Stewardship in the Kingdom of God

> **Session 3**
> Finding Your Purpose

Session 3
Finding Your Purpose

I am God's _____ and He has _____ for my life!

🔑 **Answer key**

handiwork
good works

Breakout Questions

1. How does understanding your purpose affect the way you view your finances?

2. What does it mean to you that you are God's handiwork and that he has prepared good works for you to walk in? What is one example of a good work God has called you to enter into?

Stewardship in the Kingdom of God

> **Session 3**
> Finding Your Purpose

General Purpose

Answer key

General Purpose
insignificant

All Christians have a _____. We all have a call on our lives to be a part of building God's Kingdom here on Earth. And this general calling isn't _____ .

_____
_____
_____
_____

Breakout Questions

Matthew 5:14,16 "You are the light of the world. A city set on a hill cannot be hidden... 16 Let your light shine before men in such a way that they may see your good works, and glorify your Father who is in heaven."

1. Based on this verse, what have you been called to do?

2. What are ways you can be the light of the world where you live, work and play?

Stewardship in the Kingdom of God

> **Session 3**
> Finding Your Purpose

General Purpose

You were called to let your light _____ in such a way that when people see you and the good things you are doing, they will glorify _____!

_____
_____
_____
_____

If you are a _____, you have a call to be the _____ of the world to the _____!

_____
_____
_____
_____

Answer key

shine
God
Christian
light
world

> "Take a step, step again. It is all that I can to do the next right thing. I won't look too far ahead. It's too much for me to take. But break it down to this next breath, this next step, this next choice is one that I can make." - Anna from Frozen 2

Stewardship in the Kingdom of God

> **Session 3**
> Finding Your Purpose

Personal Purpose

Answer key

General
Personal
working

God has given you more than a _____ Purpose. He has given you a _____ Purpose so that when properly _____, you will build up and grow the Body of Christ.

_____
_____
_____
_____

Individual Breakout Questions

1. As you think about things you've done, places you've volunteered, jobs you've had, what experiences have really resonated with you? What has made you come alive?

2. What have been some things that you've done, that when you've done it, it was like your inside melody was perfectly in tune with your outside environment? What have been times in your life when life felt effortless, easy, or that you were in the flow?

Stewardship in the Kingdom of God

> **Session 3**
> Finding Your Purpose

Breakout Questions

Let's share what we've reflected on in the individual breakout questions above and provide encouraging feedback to one another. This is about affirming and discovering the unique ways God has made each of us for His purposes.

"I want to caution us to not jump too quickly into _____ conclusions."

_____
_____
_____
_____

Your Personal Purpose is who you were _____ to _____, not necessarily what you were _____ to _____.

_____
_____
_____
_____

Answer key

occupational
born
be
born
do

Stewardship in the Kingdom of God

> **Session 3**
> Finding Your Purpose

Look around in your world and ask yourself this simple question: How can I be me, _____?

_____
_____
_____
_____

You'll find that there are _____ things to _____ that _____ who you were born to _____.

_____
_____
_____
_____

Answer key

here
infinite
do
support
be

Stewardship in the Kingdom of God

> **Session 3**
> Finding Your Purpose

Breakout Questions

1. What ways can you be who God created you to be in one of the contexts you currently find yourself?

2. What challenges do you face as you seek to live into WHO God created you to be?

Specific Purpose

A Specific Purpose gives us clarity on _____, _____ and _____ we are supposed to do something.

The ___ and the ____ come before the ___.

Answer key

what
when
how
G
p
s

Stewardship in the Kingdom of God

> **Session 3**
> Finding Your Purpose

Session 3 Homework

Create a visual/artistic rendering of what your life would look like if you pursued all God had for you. This is a time of digesting the words/thoughts we have had as we pause and reflect on what God has called us to do. This may be a confirmation of your general purpose, an outpouring of your personal purpose, or you may even have confirmation of the specific purpose God has for your life. The importance isn't which level of purpose you are receiving, but that you are open to the Holy Spirit leading you into all truth.

Stewardship in the Kingdom of God

> **Session 3**
> Finding Your Purpose

Passages on Spiritual Giftings

1 Corinthians 12:4-11
4 Now there are varieties of gifts, but the same Spirit. 5 And there are varieties of ministries, and the same Lord. 6 There are varieties of effects, but the same God who works all things in all persons. 7 But to each one is given the manifestation of the Spirit for the common good. 8 For to one is given the word of wisdom through the Spirit, and to another the word of knowledge according to the same Spirit; 9 to another faith by the same Spirit, and to another gifts of healing by the one Spirit, 10 and to another the effecting of miracles, and to another prophecy, and to another the distinguishing of spirits, to another various kinds of tongues, and to another the interpretation of tongues. 11 But one and the same Spirit works all these things, distributing to each one individually just as He wills.

Romans 12:6-8
6 Since we have gifts that differ according to the grace given to us, each of us is to exercise them accordingly: if prophecy, according to the proportion of his faith; 7 if service, in his serving; or he who teaches, in his teaching; 8 or he who exhorts, in his exhortation; he who gives, with liberality; he who leads, with diligence; he who shows mercy, with cheerfulness.

Ephesians 4:11-16
11 And He gave some as apostles, and some as prophets, and some as evangelists, and some as pastors and teachers, 12 for the equipping of the saints for the work of service, to the building up of the body of Christ; 13 until we all attain to the unity of the faith, and of the knowledge of the Son of God, to a mature man, to the measure of the stature which belongs to the fullness of Christ. 14 As a result, we are no longer to be children, tossed here and there by waves and carried about by every wind of doctrine, by the trickery of men, by craftiness in deceitful scheming; 15 but speaking the truth in love, we are to grow up in all aspects into Him who is the head, even Christ, 16 from whom the whole body, being fitted and held together by what every joint supplies, according to the proper working of each individual part, causes the growth of the body for the building up of itself in love.

INCREASE

4

Session 4
Roadblocks to Finding Your Purpose

Christians stop pursuing their purpose because of lack of clarity, shut doors, and limited thinking. How do we know what we are called to? Or if we feel called, how can we be certain of our purpose? When doors get shut in our face, should we break the door down or see it as a divine redirect? Are we putting our own limitations on God as we evaluate our calling? With God, all things are possible. We must determine what those "all things" are for us individually and pursue them unencumbered.

General Personal Specific

G   P   S

Stewardship in the Kingdom of God

Session 4
Roadblocks to Finding Your Purpose

_____ is the _____ to _____.

Answer key

Community
key
success

Breakout Questions

Present vision boards, artistic renderings, and the dreams you have for your life. Share those with your people, and after each one, celebrate their GPS Direction!

Roadblock #1: Lack of Clarity

Clarity is a _____ and not a _____ .

Answer key

journey
destination

Stewardship in the Kingdom of God

> **Session 4**
> Roadblocks to Finding Your Purpose

🔑 **Answer key**

confidence
reliance

Faith allows us to move forward in _____ and _____.

_____
_____
_____
_____
_____

Faith in God and His purposes for our lives.

Faith that...

- God is good, knows what He is doing, and has PERFECT timing.
- Even if we don't know where this all leads, we believe God has given us everything we need for life and godliness in this moment and in this season.
- God's ways are not our ways, but His ways are best.
- Only knowing one step is sometimes enough.
- God is for you and not against you.
- Even though you don't see a specific purpose for your life today, you are God's workmanship, His handiwork, His prized creation.
- He who began a good work in you will carry it on to completion until the day of Christ Jesus.
- As you steward your general and personal purposes, your specific purposes will come to fruition in your life.
- Is the key that allows us to move forward in full confidence and humble reliance.

Stewardship in the Kingdom of God

> **Session 4**
> Roadblocks to Finding Your Purpose

Roadblock #2: SHUT DOORS

When doors get shut in our face, should we break the door _____ or see it as a divine _____?

_____ _____ helps open a conversation.

"When doors are closed, should I knock them _____ or see them as _____ _____?"

Answer key

- down
- redirect
- Asking questions
- down
- divine redirects

Session 04 // 12. Page 46

Stewardship in the Kingdom of God

Session 4
Roadblocks to Finding Your Purpose

Breakout Questions

1. What doors are shut for you right now that are stopping you from pursuing your GPS? Discuss with the group if you believe you should see it as a divine redirect or an opportunity to break a door down.

2. If you believe a door that looks closed should be pounded on or knocked down, what is one action you can take and how can your group members pray for you?

Stewardship in the Kingdom of God

Session 4
Roadblocks to Finding Your Purpose

Roadblock #3: Limited Thinking

God changes _____ to change _____.

_____
_____
_____
_____

We have _____ we need through our _____ of _____!

_____
_____
_____
_____

Answer key

lives
lives
everything
knowledge
Him

INCREASE

5

Session 5
The Necessity of a Sustainable Financial System

Too many people start a new fad and it fades. When it comes to personal finance, there's always a new solution, a new guru, or a new problem that you are solving. We need a sustainable solution for our personal finances that doesn't fade and that is connected to our purpose. Christians should be the best stewards of money because we know Whose money we are stewarding!

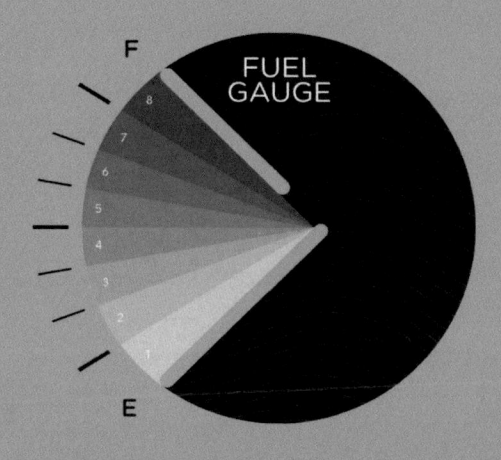

Stewardship in the Kingdom of God

Session 5
The Necessity of a Sustainable Financial System

> "Money targets that are devoid of purpose targets, and not connected to the life God has for us are futile and evil. To pursue money in and of itself is dangerous at best and completely destructive at worst."

Our mindset towards money, and our understanding of money's _____ is crucial for practically _____ our finances effectively.

_____
_____
_____
_____

Answer key

purpose
stewarding

Stewardship in the Kingdom of God

> Session 5
> The Necessity of a Sustainable Financial System

Part 1: A city on a hill that doesn't dim

_____ should be the best _____ of money because we know _____ money we are _____!

_____
_____
_____
_____

There is a _____ to the _____ of God in our lives.

_____
_____
_____
_____

Answer key

important
long
purposes
longevity
stewarding
Whose
stewards
Christians

The purposes of God in our life are as _____ as they are _____.

_____
_____
_____
_____

"Once the car is cleaned and ready, I do the most important part of our prep. I drive to the nearest gas station at our house and **I fill our tank to full.**"

Stewardship in the Kingdom of God

Session 5
The Necessity of a Sustainable Financial System

Part 2: F.U.E.L. Gauge

> "This F.U.E.L. Gauge will ensure you're not constantly worried about that line hitting empty and it will give you the marks you need to hit to fill your tank full. In our personal finances, there are 8 marks on our F.U.E.L. Gauge that give us an indication of what we have in the tank."

8 Marks of our F.U.E.L. Gauge

8/8 Housing at 25%

7/8 New Zero in Savings

6/8 Invest 15%

5/8 Consumer Debt Paid Off

4/8 Adequate Insurance

3/8 New Zero in Checking

2/8 Give 10%

1/8 Balanced Budget

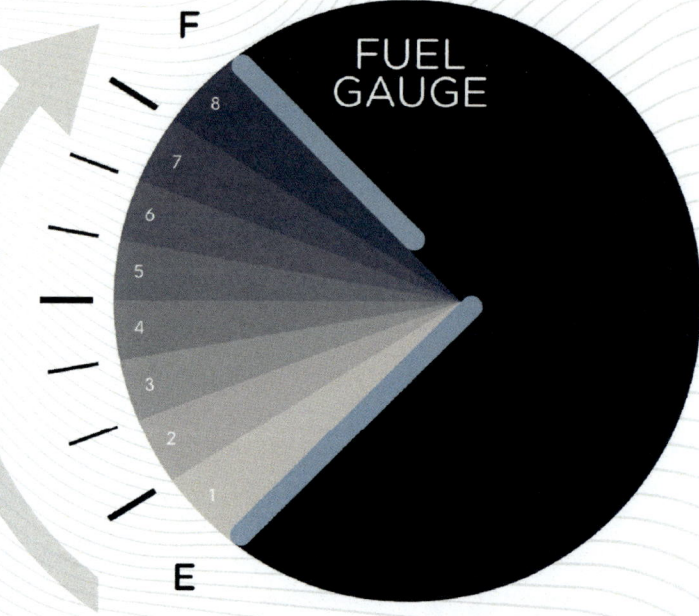

Stewardship in the Kingdom of God

Session 5
The Necessity of a Sustainable Financial System

In accounting terms, our F.U.E.L Check will help us both _____ and _____.

A budget is _____ _____.

Budgets project out, typically one month at a time, and provide guide _____ for _____ so that we have an idea of where we are going to be using our money and areas we should avoid _____.

An _____ ensures that you did what you said you would do, that you stuck to your budget.

Answer key

audit
budget
forward looking
rails
spending
overspending
audit

Stewardship in the Kingdom of God

> **Session 5**
> The Necessity of a Sustainable Financial System

Completing the monthly F.U.E.L Check as close to the beginning of the _____ as possible allows you to look completely at the previous month while also making _____ to the current month before anything gets too far away from you.

The F.U.E.L. Check

Answer key

month
tweaks
Finalize
Unleash

F _____ Budget: Audit last month and make any adjustments to this month.

U _____ God's Direction: Pray, thanking God for where you're at and asking for His divine wisdom and provision over your finances.

Stewardship in the Kingdom of God

Session 5
The Necessity of a Sustainable Financial System

E _____: where you are at on your F.U.E.L. Gauge.

_____
_____
_____
_____

L _____ _____: What will you do this month to move towards your next mark?

_____
_____
_____
_____

Prioritize your energy and your resources into ensuring that you are consistently hitting each mark _____ before moving towards the next mark. When you do, your _____ will provide _____ and _____ growth.

_____
_____
_____
_____

Answer key

Evaluate
Look Forward
in order
consistency
stability
predictable

F.U.E.L. Check Roles

The Driver's Role
- Executes the plan.
- Performs the monthly F.U.E.L. Check.
- Ensure you are making forward progress towards the next mark until the tank is full.
- Responsible for communicating any changes they are proposing and getting agreement and buy-in from their spouse before finalizing their budget.

The Role of Riding Shotgun
- Stay engaged in the financial lessons.
- See danger ahead, encourage the driver, and support the driver as they make sure you're on track each month.
- Don't be a backseat driver!
- Be ready to take the wheel if the driver needs a break.

Important notes on roles
- **Trust and Communication:** Essential for effective financial management; the Driver needs trust and open communication with the person Riding Shotgun for confident decision-making.
- **Flexibility in Role Dynamics:** Roles of Driver and Riding Shotgun are adaptable and not gender-specific; they can be assumed by either partner based on skills and preferences, allowing for role switching as life circumstances change.
- **Collaborative Decision Making:** Joint financial decisions are crucial for a unified approach, ensuring both partners are aligned and committed.
- **Visibility and Preventive Insight:** The Person Riding Shotgun provides crucial oversight, spotting potential financial challenges and opportunities, reinforcing the plan.
- **Shared Responsibility and Unity:** Both partners share the responsibility for financial planning, promoting unity in goals and values for a harmonious financial journey.

Stewardship in the Kingdom of God

> **Session 5**
> The Necessity of a Sustainable Financial System

Breakout Questions

1. Growing up, what financial issues or subjects caused the most tension in your home?

2. What has been your experience as an adult when you've discussed money with your spouse or loved ones?

3. How do you feel about one spouse being responsible for Driving and one spouse actively Riding Shotgun? And why do you feel that way?

4. What things need to be true for you to feel you can fully trust your spouse in their role?

Stewardship in the Kingdom of God

> Session 5
> The Necessity of a Sustainable Financial System

Breakout Questions

5. Designate one spouse as the Driver in the box below. If you're single, put your name in the Driver's seat!

DRIVER:

8 Marks of our F.U.E.L. Gauge

8/8 Housing at 25%

7/8 New Zero in Savings

6/8 Invest 15%

5/8 Consumer Debt Paid Off

4/8 Adequate Insurance

3/8 New Zero in Checking

2/8 Give 10%

1/8 Balanced Budget

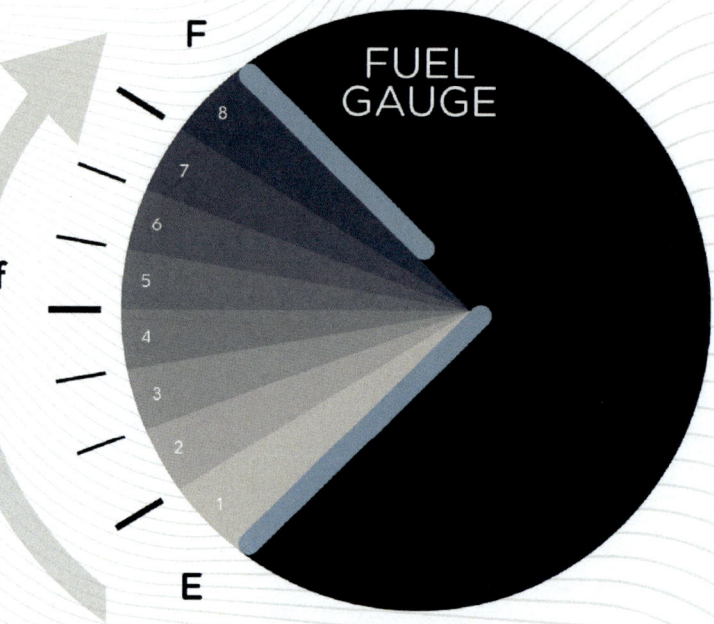

Stewardship in the Kingdom of God

> **Session 5**
> The Necessity of a Sustainable Financial System

Breakout Question

What lessons about operating the F.U.E.L. Check can you extract from Jackie's journey? Make a list and share those with the group.

Breakout Questions

1. How will your month-to-month mindset change when you know that you have a full tank?

2. What will having a full tank allow you and your family to do?

Stewardship in the Kingdom of God

> **Session 5**
> The Necessity of a Sustainable Financial System

Session 5 Homework

Your homework for this session is easy:

1. Affirm your decision for who will be the Driver.

DRIVER:

2. Spend some more time going over our first round of discussion questions listed below. Don't breeze over these. Take time to have a cup of coffee with your spouse or a friend and unpack how your upbringing has shaped how you view money in the home.
   - Growing up, what financial issues or subjects caused the most tension in your home?
   - What has been your experience as an adult when you've discussed money with your spouse or loved ones?
   - How do you feel about one spouse being responsible for Driving and one spouse actively Riding Shotgun? And why do you feel that way?
   - What things need to be true for you to feel you can fully trust your spouse in their role?

INCREASE

6

Session 6
Increase Your Income

Stewarding your finances isn't just making sure that you are in the "black" every month. We are called to steward increase. Part of leaning into stewarding the life God has given you is stewarding the value you are bringing to the work you are doing. We must not be content with being the same and offering the same value. We must increase our value, and thereby increase our income.

Session 6
Increase Your Income

Stewardship in the Kingdom of God

> "Achieving a full tank is most likely not going to be possible with the income you're currently making. Many financial courses will teach you how to properly allocate the money that you bring in each month. Many Christians even call this proper allocation, stewardship. But we've learned through our study of Scripture that stewardship requires increase. Yes, we must be content, but we must also work to increase the resources God has entrusted to us."

Instead of trading _____ for _____ , we're going to learn how to trade _____ for _____ .

_____
_____
_____
_____

Answer key

time
money
value
money

Stewardship in the Kingdom of God

> **Session 6**
> Increase Your Income

Income Target Calculation

Objective: Determine your income target based on your housing expenses to ensure your housing costs are 25% of your take-home pay.

Step 1: Calculate Required Take-Home Pay

- **Formula:** Housing Expense ÷ 0.25 = Required Take-Home Pay
- **Example:**
  - If your monthly mortgage is $2,200, then:
  - $2,200 ÷ 0.25 = $8,800
- **Your Housing Expense:** $_____ ÷ 0.25 = $_____ (Required Take-Home Pay)

Step 2: Determine Top-Line Income Target

- Considering an average tax deduction of 25%, calculate the gross income needed.
- **Formula:** Required Take-Home Pay ÷ 0.75 = Top-Line Income Target
- **Example:**
  - $8,800 ÷ 0.75 = $11,733
- **Your Required Take-Home Pay:** $_____ ÷ 0.75 = $_____ (Top-Line Income Target)

Step 3: Annualize Your Income Target

- To find out your yearly income target, multiply your monthly Top-Line Income Target by 12.
- **Example:**
  - $11,733 x 12 = $140,796 (Annual Income Target)
- **Your Top-Line Income Target:** $_____ x 12 = $_____ (Annual Income Target)

Note: This calculation assumes a standard tax rate of 25%. Your actual tax rate may vary. Adjust the formula if you have precise tax rate information.

Stewardship in the Kingdom of God

Session 6
Increase Your Income

_____ creates _____.

Answer key

Perspective
possibility

Breakout Questions

1. What roadblocks do you foresee as you think about increasing your income?

2. If someone else in the group has ever faced those roadblocks, how did you work through them or how are you working through them now?

Stewardship in the Kingdom of God

Session 6
Increase Your Income

Step 1: Abide in Jesus

John 15:5 says, "I am the _____ and you are the _____. He who _____ in me and I in him will bear much fruit for apart from me you can do nothing."

_____
_____
_____
_____

Meaningful _____ always begins with _____.

_____
_____
_____
_____

Self-reliance is a _____ of _____.

_____
_____
_____
_____

Answer key

vine
branches
abides
increase
prayer
thief
potential

Stewardship in the Kingdom of God

Session 6
Increase Your Income

Breakout Questions

1. Where in your life are you operating in your own power? What are areas in your life that lack prayer and therefore show self reliance?

Step 2: Understand Your Value

The best way to make more money where you are at is by understanding the _____ you're _____ to the organization and how to _____ that _____.

_____
_____
_____
_____

Answer key

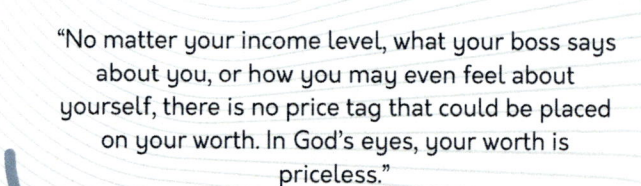

value
increase
bringing
value

> "No matter your income level, what your boss says about you, or how you may even feel about yourself, there is no price tag that could be placed on your worth. In God's eyes, your worth is priceless."

Stewardship in the Kingdom of God

Session 6
Increase Your Income

Your _____ has a price tag. _____ in the marketplace means _____.

_____
_____
_____
_____

There's only value in the _____ inasmuch as it helps the _____ or the _____.

_____
_____
_____
_____

After all of the expenses are subtracted from the total revenue, or the top line, you're left with your bottom line, your _____ or _____.

_____
_____
_____
_____

Answer key

Value
Value
cold hard cash
marketplace
top line
bottom line
profit
surplus

Stewardship in the Kingdom of God

> **Session 6**
> Increase Your Income

Breakout Questions

1. What work do you do and does it increase the revenue of the organization, or decrease expenses, or a combination of the two and why?

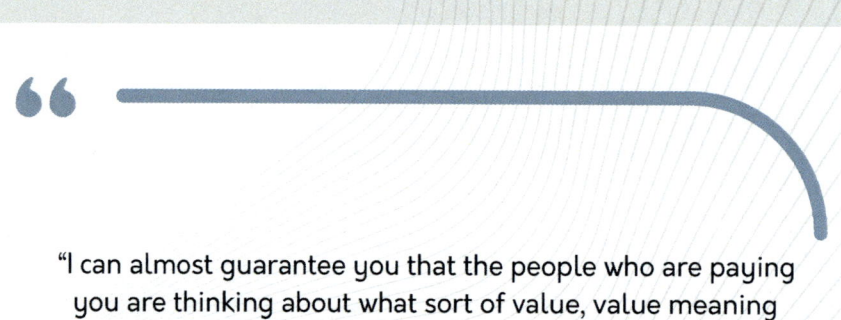

> "I can almost guarantee you that the people who are paying you are thinking about what sort of value, value meaning cold hard cash, you are bringing to the organization."

By asking how you can increase your _____, you are positioning yourself as a _____ _____ for _____ and _____.

_____
_____
_____
_____

Answer key

value
prime candidate
promotions
raises

Stewardship in the Kingdom of God

Session 6
Increase Your Income

Step 3: Increase your Purpose

Every moment of every day isn't going to be _____, but you should feel that the work you are doing is in _____ with the sort of person you are _____.

Answer key

euphoric
line
becoming

Practical Ways to Increase your Value in the Marketplace

1. **Education**
   - Focus on application, not just volume of knowledge.
   - Practice reading or listening to books that resonate with you and apply their teachings.
   - Recommended reads:
     - "The Energy Bus" by Jon Gordon for positivity and attitude.
     - "Good to Great" by Jim Collins for translating business principles to personal growth.
     - "No is a Beautiful Word" by Kevin Harney for learning the power of saying "No."
   - Consider industry designations for specific expertise and knowledge.

2. **Mentors and Coaches**
   - Utilize books and resources from experts like John Maxwell and Zig Ziglar as virtual coaches.
   - Seek mentors who have achieved goals similar to yours for guidance and modeling.
   - As value increases, consider professional coaching and ask your organization to support this growth.

Breakout Questions

1. What is one step you can take today to increase your value to your organization?

Stewardship in the Kingdom of God

> **Session 6**
> Increase Your Income

Session 6 Homework

1. Schedule a conversation with your boss or a key leader in your organization. Ask how you can work to increase your value to the organization and how your work contributes to the top or bottom line. Let them know your income target and ask them what you would need to do in order to hit that target in your organization.

2. Spend time in prayer, seeking God's direction for your finances.

2. Plan your next step. What next step will you take to move towards your income target?

INCREASE

Session 7
1/8th - Balanced Budget

You have a beautiful future. One that you are motivated to live into and work towards. But where are you today? Are you on the right path financially? Do you have enough fuel in the tank to get there? If you don't know your money, your money won't know you. As you audit what you know about your finances, you'll begin to see leaks, areas of your budget that are causing cash to drain out of your accounts. We don't need to panic about every area of our budget, but we do need to correct the glaring holes if we want to make any headway towards our goals.

Stewardship in the Kingdom of God

Session 7
1/8th - Balanced Budget

F.U.E.L. Gauge Review

The 8 Marks of our F.U.E.L. Gauge

8/8 Housing at 25%

7/8 New Zero in Savings

6/8 Invest 15%

5/8 Consumer Debt Paid Off

4/8 Adequate Insurance

3/8 New Zero in Checking

2/8 Give 10%

1/8 Balanced Budget

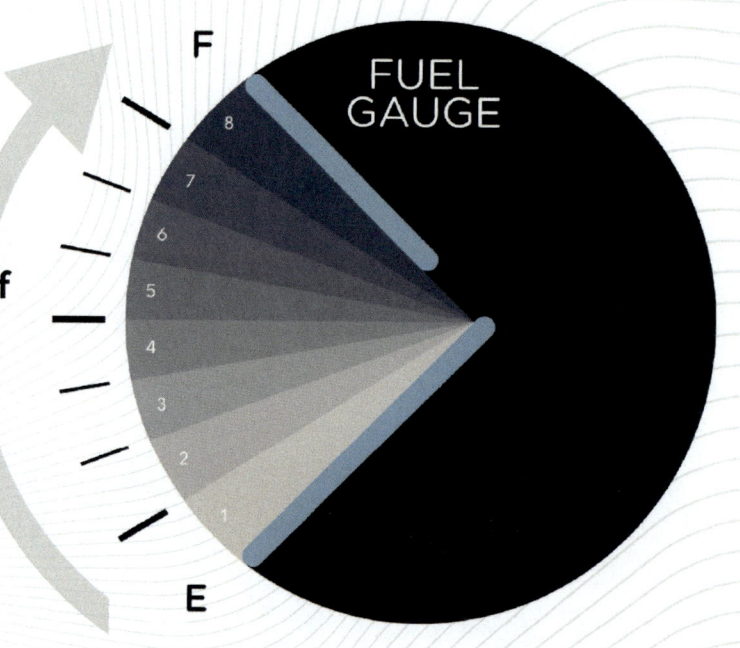

If we can fully understand _____ we are doing something, we're much more likely to _____ to doing it for the long term.

Answer key

why
stick

Stewardship in the Kingdom of God

Session 7
1/8th – Balanced Budget

Part 1: Face the Music

	BEST GUESS	RIGHT NOW	THIS MONTH
Income			
Take home pay	_____	_____	_____
Take home pay	_____	_____	_____
Total	_____	_____	_____
Expenses			
Retirement	_____	_____	_____
Giving/Generosity	_____	_____	_____
Mortgage/Rent	_____	_____	_____
Car Payment	_____	_____	_____
Other Debt	_____	_____	_____
Insurance	_____	_____	_____
Utilities	_____	_____	_____
Auto/Gas	_____	_____	_____
Groceries	_____	_____	_____
Eating Out	_____	_____	_____
Entertainment	_____	_____	_____
Household Items	_____	_____	_____
Subscriptions	_____	_____	_____
Other _____	_____	_____	_____
Other _____	_____	_____	_____
Other _____	_____	_____	_____
Total	_____	_____	_____
Cash Flow (+/-)	_____	_____	_____

Stewardship in the Kingdom of God

Session 7
1/8th - Balanced Budget

Here's the principle: sort your _____ into _____ on a _____ basis.

_____
_____
_____
_____

Part 2: Stop the Bleeding

More than likely, there's only _____ or _____ small areas of your budget that are out of control, and if I had to guess, the rest of your budget isn't that bad. All is not lost.

_____
_____
_____
_____

Tool #1: Cashball

Answer key

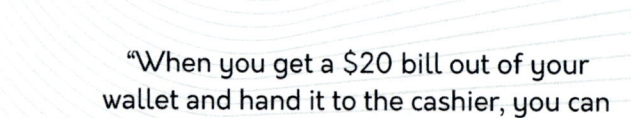

two
one
monthly
categories
expenses

> "When you get a $20 bill out of your wallet and hand it to the cashier, you can actually feel that money leaving you."

Stewardship in the Kingdom of God

Session 7
1/8th - Balanced Budget

Cash is a definite solution for stopping the bleeding in
_ _ _ _ _ _ or _ _ _ _ _ categories of your budget.

Answer key

one
two

Breakout Questions

1. As you look at your "Best Guess" budget, even before auditing it, do you know one or two areas of your spending that are out of control? What are they and why do you think they are hard for you to keep under control?

2. What is one area of your budget that you think using cash for would help you be a more conscious spender?

Stewardship in the Kingdom of God

Session 7
1/8th – Balanced Budget

Tool #2: 24-Hour Pause

The _____ puts an appropriate amount of _____ on your transaction if online shopping is an area of weakness for you.

_____
_____
_____
_____

Answer key

24-hour pause
friction

Breakout Questions

1. Talk about a time you rushed into making a purchase because it was easy or because you felt like you were up against the clock.

2. Do you or someone you know struggle with retail therapy? What causes you to spend and how might practicing the 24 hour pause improve your ability to stay within your budget?

Stewardship in the Kingdom of God

Session 7
1/8th – Balanced Budget

Tool #3: Buddy System

If cash doesn't work and you don't have the will power to pause, it's time to get other people _____ in stopping your bank account from being drained.

Answer key

involved

Session 7 Homework

For this session's homework, we'll continue to face the music by auditing your "Best Guess" budget to create your "Right Now Budget" on page 75.

1. Face the Music: Audit your Best Guess Budget.
2. Underline one, two, or three areas of your budget where you're spending is way out of whack. Set a realistic budget for that category. Determine which tool you are going to use to stop the bleeding and stay within your set budget for this coming month.
3. If your budget is not balanced, meaning your take home pay isn't greater than or equal to your budgeted expenses, determine what "nice to have things" need to be cut in order to create a balanced budget for this upcoming month. We will get into having a balanced budget more in depth in weeks to come, but for now, be proactive and see what areas you can cut back if your expenses are more than your income.

Session 7
1/8th – Balanced Budget

Stewardship in the Kingdom of God

INCREASE

8

Session 8
2/8 – Give 10%
3/8 – New Zero in Checking
4/8 – Adequate Insurance

We must have a healthy and biblical view of Whose money we are stewarding. If we begin every month by giving 10% of all we earn, the other 90% of our budget will be viewed and spent appropriately. Every builder knows that before they build their dream house, they must first lay the appropriate foundation. If Christians begin going after their dreams without first laying a financial foundation, everything they are working for could crumble in the blink of an eye. Having a cushion in your checking account and the appropriate insurance in place are key components of a solid financial foundation.

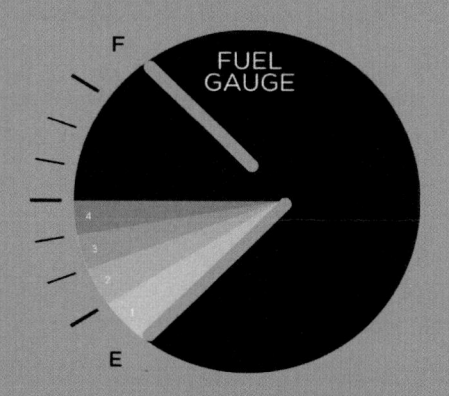

Stewardship in the Kingdom of God

> **Session 8**
> 2/8 - Give 10%, 3/8 - New Zero in Checking, 4/8 - Adequate Insurance

Take Home Pay

A balanced budget is spending _____ to or _____ than your TAKE HOME PAY.

_____
_____
_____
_____

The number that hits your bank account often has several _____ that come out in between your employer's hand and your wallet.

_____
_____
_____
_____

Answer key

equal
less
expenses
engineer
paychecks
add back

The easiest way to calculate take home pay is to reverse _____ your paycheck or if you have multiple incomes, your _____. When looking at your pay stub, simply take the money that hits your account and _____ _____ in any of your retirement contributions and insurance expenses.

_____
_____
_____
_____

Stewardship in the Kingdom of God

> **Session 8**
> 2/8 – Give 10%, 3/8 – New Zero in Checking, 4/8 – Adequate Insurance

Sample Pay Stub

Pay Period: Nov. 1st - Nov. 15th	Pay Date: November 15th
Earnings and Hours	
Salary	**3,000.00**
Deductions from Gross	
401k Emp.	- 450.00
Health Ins. Emp.	- 210.00
Total	**- 660.00**
Taxes	
Federal Withholding	- 236.00
Social Security Emp.	- 186.00
Medicare Emp.	- 43.50
State Withholding	- 137.20
Total	**- 602.70**
Net Pay	1.737.30

Breakout Questions

Determine your Take Home Pay (See Below). Since you have already audited your take home pay from last month, determine your budgeted take home pay for this upcoming month. Make any tweaks that you deem necessary as you project your Take Home Pay for the upcoming month's budget.

Stewardship in the Kingdom of God

> **Session 8**
2/8 - Give 10%, 3/8 - New Zero in Checking, 4/8 - Adequate Insurance

Calculating Take Home Pay

Net Amount Deposited to Your Account   _____

Add Back:

Retirement Contributions: + _____

Insurance Expenses   + _____

Total Take Home Pay   = _____

10% - Giving

Giving away the first 10% of what you make is not _____. Giving from your first fruits is _____ and _____ our hearts with God's heart.

_____
_____
_____
_____

Answer key

generosity
obedience
aligns
lean not
understanding

Giving 10% of our first fruits is a very practical way for us to _____ on our own _____.

_____
_____
_____
_____
_____

Stewardship in the Kingdom of God

Session 8
2/8 – Give 10%, 3/8 – New Zero in Checking, 4/8 – Adequate Insurance

Giving 10% of our first fruits is a practical means of _____ God in _____ of our ways.

_____
_____
_____
_____

Answer key

90%
tone
all
Acknowledging

Giving 10% of our income at the very beginning of each month sets the _____ for the rest of the _____ of our budget

_____
_____
_____
_____

Breakout Questions

1. How have you seen giving become a religious habit devoid of a God-honoring heart connection?

Session 08 // 12. Page 85

Stewardship in the Kingdom of God

Session 8
2/8 – Give 10%, 3/8 – New Zero in Checking, 4/8 – Adequate Insurance

2. Why does God want us to give from our first fruits? What message do we send to God and the world if we give from our leftovers and make giving the last thing on our financial checklist?

New Checking Zero

I decided to save up one _____ of my expenses and told myself that when I saw that number in my checking account, I was _____. That number was what I called my _____ _____.

Answer key

month
broke
New Zero

Calculating Your New Checking Zero

Step 1: Total Expenses from your "Right Now Budget" (e.g. $4,526)

$ _____

Step 2: Round up to the nearest $1,000 (e.g. $4,526 -> $5,000)

$ _____

Our New Checking Zero $ _____

Stewardship in the Kingdom of God

Session 8
2/8 – Give 10%, 3/8 – New Zero in Checking, 4/8 – Adequate Insurance

First, agree to a balanced _____, then agree to giving ____ inside of that balanced budget, and third, agree to your _____.

_____
_____
_____
_____

As you're saving money to fund your New Zero and once you have fully funded it, agree that under no circumstances will you spend that money for discretionary purchases.

_____
_____
_____
_____

Answer key

budget
10%
New Checking Zero

Stewardship in the Kingdom of God

Session 8
2/8 – Give 10%, 3/8 – New Zero in Checking, 4/8 – Adequate Insurance

New Checking Zero Agreements

In committing to the path towards Increase, I agree to the following terms:

I Agree to Maintain a Balanced Budget.
- I agree to regularly review and balance our budget to ensure it aligns with our G.P.S.

I Agree to Give 10%.
- I agree to allocate 10% of our income towards giving, to align our hearts with God's heart.

I Agree to Adhere to the New Checking Zero Target.
- I agree to set and adhere to the New Checking Zero target, ensuring that our spending aligns with our G.P.S.

I Agree Not to Use New Checking Zero Funds for Discretionary Purchases.
- While saving for our New Zero, I agree not to use funds from our New Checking Zero for non-essential, discretionary purchases.

Signature: _____ Date: _____

Signature: _____ Date: _____

Stewardship in the Kingdom of God

> **Session 8**
2/8 – Give 10%, 3/8 – New Zero in Checking, 4/8 – Adequate Insurance

Breakout Questions

1. When you have had extra money in savings, how has that made you feel? Did your savings provide a sense of peace or do you feel that money is meant to be used and spent?

2. Do you trust yourself to keep your New Checking Zero funded or are you scared that the money will grow wings and fly away? What experiences have led you to feel this way?

Adequate Insurance

Insurance: taking a small financial _____ now, so that later, you don't have to potentially take a _____ financial loss.

Answer key

larger
loss

Stewardship in the Kingdom of God

Session 8
2/8 - Give 10%, 3/8 - New Zero in Checking, 4/8 - Adequate Insurance

Some people _____ afford to not have insurance.

But for the rest of us, we _____ afford to _____ have insurance.

Another way that you self insure risk is through _____.

"I don't want to pay a penny _____ to an insurance company than I have to, however, I also can't afford to pay a penny _____ than I should."

Answer key

- less
- more
- deductibles
- NOT
- CAN'T
- CAN

Stewardship in the Kingdom of God

Session 8
2/8 – Give 10%, 3/8 – New Zero in Checking, 4/8 – Adequate Insurance

Everyone needs four basic insurance policies: _____, _____, _____, and _____.

Answer key

Home
Auto
Health
Life

Homeowners Insurance

For items that are particularly _____ such as jewelry, collectibles, heirlooms, guns, or recreational vehicles, it is important to talk with your agent about what is and what is not covered for those items. If you have special collections of _____ or other _____, make sure to discuss what coverage is and isn't provided on a standard homeowners policy and if there are any additional coverages you should consider purchasing.

Answer key

valuable
memorabilia
valuables

Stewardship in the Kingdom of God

> **Session 8**
> 2/8 - Give 10%, 3/8 - New Zero in Checking, 4/8 - Adequate Insurance

Auto Insurance

🔒
Answer key

property
casualty

Just like the homeowner's policy, there is _____ and _____ insurance on the auto policy.

_____
_____
_____
_____

Health Insurance

🔒
Answer key

deductible
plan type

Your _____ and _____ _____ are the most important things to FULLY understand when choosing the right health insurance.

_____
_____
_____
_____

Life Insurance

🔒
Answer key

10-20 times
annual

"I recommend purchasing between _____ your _____ income on a term life insurance policy."

_____
_____
_____
_____

Stewardship in the Kingdom of God

Session 8
2/8 - Give 10%, 3/8 - New Zero in Checking, 4/8 - Adequate Insurance

At a ____ return, your family would be able to live off of the interest, which at ____ of _____ times your income happens to be equal to your current annual _____.

Answer key
(upside down)
income
20
5%
5%

Session 8 Homework

Now for this session's homework, we'll be focusing on the three concepts we learned today: Giving, Your "New Zero" in Checking, and Adequate Insurance.

1. Working through the steps on your Fuel Gauge is personal and should be done at your own pace. If you just balanced your budget for the first time this past week, begin thinking about how much you'll be able to give this next month.

Stewardship in the Kingdom of God

Session 8
2/8 – Give 10%, 3/8 – New Zero in Checking, 4/8 – Adequate Insurance

2. Discuss the concept of the New Checking Zero. Talk about any fears or concerns you may have with having a cushion sitting in plane sight in your checking account. Commit to yourself and to one another if you're married that you'll see your New Zero as a new baseline, money that you will not spend except for in the event of emergencies.

3. List your Homeowners Insurance, Auto Insurance, Health Insurance, and Life Insurance policies and deductibles. Are these policies adequate? Consult an expert if you're unsure!

Policy Type	Provider	Deductible(s)	Adequate? (Y/N)
Homeowners Insurance			
Auto Insurance			
Health Insurance			
Life Insurance #1			
Life Insurance #2 (if applicable)			

INCREASE

9

Session 9
5/8 – Consumer Debt

Debt can be a destructive evil or a useful tool – it's all in how you understand assets. Debt that is backed by an asset can be useful if used properly for your home, your vehicle, and business, and in some cases, your education. In this section, we lay out guidelines on useful and harmful debt and how to ensure you never dig a hole bigger than the assets that are backing it. In this section, we also work to eliminate consumer debt which has hamstrung many Christians from pursuing all God has for them.

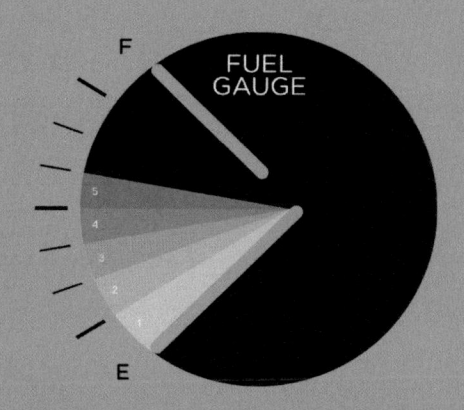

Stewardship in the Kingdom of God

> Session 9
5/8 – Consumer Debt

Debt is Neither Right Nor Wrong

Answer key

wisdom
sin

Debt is neither right nor wrong. Debt is not a _ _ _ _ _ issue, debt is a _ _ _ _ _ _ _ _ _ _ _ issue.

Debt is a wisdom issue!

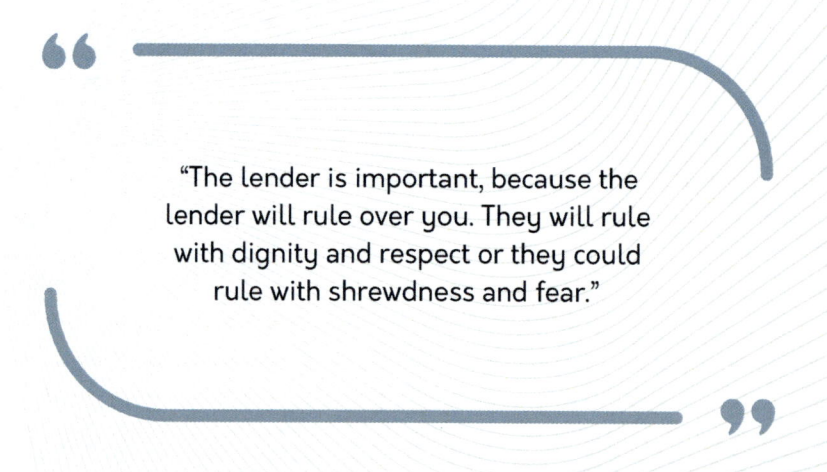

> "The lender is important, because the lender will rule over you. They will rule with dignity and respect or they could rule with shrewdness and fear."

Proverbs 22:26-27: "Be not one of those who give pledges, who put up security for debts. If you have nothing with which to pay, why should your bed be taken from under you?"

Proverbs 17:18: "One who lacks sense gives a pledge and promises security in the presence of his neighbor."

Stewardship in the Kingdom of God

Session 9
5/8 – Consumer Debt

Encouraging your child to get qualified for a _____ on their own may take longer, but to _____ simply to rush the buying process is _____ and _____.

Answer key

loan
co-sign
unwise
premature

Repay What is Owed

Romans 13:7-8:, "give to everyone what you owe them... Let no debt remain outstanding."

As long as it is up to you, work to _____ what is _____ so that no _____ is left _____.

Answer key

repay
owed
debt
outstanding

Stewardship in the Kingdom of God

> **Session 9**
5/8 – Consumer Debt

Debt isn't a substitute for hard work!

Proverbs 21:5 "The plans of the diligent lead surely to abundance, but everyone who is hasty comes only to poverty."

Answer key

hard work
hard work

Debt should not take the place of _____ _____. As you consider borrowing money, do so alongside _____ _____.

_____
_____
_____
_____

Breakout Questions

1. How have you viewed debt in the past and how has your view changed over time?

2. What is the difference between debt being a sin issue and a wisdom issue?

3. Share one of the guiding principles we discussed about using wisdom in managing debt. How did you find it particularly helpful?

Forms of Debt

> "Debt is a wisdom issue. I neither am for or against debt. I believe that debt is situational and requires substantial consideration from the borrower."

Imagine you are in your backyard and you have a shovel. You decide you're going to _____ a _____ big enough for a pool. This is like taking on _____.

In the first scenario, the dirt beside the hole represents an _____. If you can't afford the mortgage, you sell the house - the dirt _____ the hole.

Answer key

(upside down:)
- dig
- hole
- debt
- asset-backed debt
- fills

Stewardship in the Kingdom of God

Session 9
5/8 - Consumer Debt

In the second scenario, where the dirt is taken away, this represents _____ _____. Like using a credit card for a vacation - once spent, it's gone, leaving a_____ _____.

_____
_____
_____
_____

Answer key

unsecured debt
financial hole

Consumer Debt

What matters is that you _____ every leftover penny each month towards _____ in this _____.

_____
_____
_____
_____

If you feel you are maximizing your _____, then as a second step, you can begin to _____ your hours.

_____
_____
_____
_____

Answer key

allocate
filling
hole
value
increase

Stewardship in the Kingdom of God

Session 9
5/8 – Consumer Debt

If you have held a _____ _____ balance and need to pay off consumer debt, you need to be consumer debt free for _____ _____ before I recommend even touching another credit card.

Answer key

credit card
one year

Student Loans

All student loans are not _____ equal because the education they are purchasing is not created _____.

A college degree isn't a _____ for _____. A college degree can certainly be helpful, but if it requires you to dig a hole _____ than you'll be able to reasonably fill in, it is not worth going into _____.

Answer key

debt
deeper
success
prerequisite
equal
created

Stewardship in the Kingdom of God

Session 9
5/8 - Consumer Debt

Paying _____ for college is always best. Even if you can't _____ for all of it, _____ _____ and get as many _____ as you can.

_____
_____
_____
_____

Answer key
- cash
- pay
- work hard
- scholarships

Car Loans

Cars are _____ assets. The pile of dirt beside your hole keeps getting smaller and smaller, often _____ than you are paying back the loan.

_____
_____
_____
_____

If you do not have a _____ _____ and every mark on your _____ _____ isn't completed, then I do not recommend auto loans.

_____
_____
_____
_____

Answer key
- depreciating
- faster
- full tank
- Fuel Gauge

Stewardship in the Kingdom of God

Session 9
5/8 – Consumer Debt

If you decide on an _____ _____, never take one bigger than your _____.

Answer key

auto loan
New Savings Zero

Mortgages

When purchasing a home, your target is to get your monthly mortgage payment within _____ of your _____.

For first-time home buyers, we recommend a _____ with as much down as you can muster, ideally _____ down to eliminate mortgage insurance.

Answer key

25%
take home pay
30 year mortgage
20%

Stewardship in the Kingdom of God

Session 9
5/8 – Consumer Debt

If you can afford a _____ on the house you'd like while staying within the _____, we wholeheartedly recommend it to pay less _____ and be rid of your mortgage in _____ of the time.

Answer key
- 15 year mortgage
- 25%
- interest
- half

Breakout Questions

1. Discuss the difference between unsecured debt and asset backed debt. How are they different? Use Zach's analogy if needed as you talk about the differences.

2. How have you seen consumer debt be a trap that has pulled people down and harmed them financially?

Session 9 Homework
The Giving Challenge

Step 1: Withdraw and Prepare:

- Head to the bank and withdraw a crisp $100 bill. If you're married, each partner should withdraw $100. If $100 is not feasible, opt for $20 or $50, but ensure to withdraw some amount.
- Place this money in your wallet or purse, ready for the next step.

Step 2: Identify the Recipient:

- In prayer and reflection, consider who in your circle could benefit from this act of kindness. This gift should be for an individual or a family, not an organization.

Step 3: Make the Connection:

- When you have identified the recipient, don't just hand over the money and leave. Engage in a meaningful conversation, sharing that this is a blessing from God, utilizing you as a channel for His generosity.

Guidelines:

- Ensure the gift is personal and to someone you can see face-to-face.
- Embrace this as an opportunity for God to work through you.
- Focus on blessing and encouraging the recipient where they are at in their life.

INCREASE

10

Session 10

6/8 – Invest 15%
7/8 – New Zero in Savings
8/8 – Housing at 25%

After consumer debt is paid off, it's time to begin investing 15% of our take home pay for retirement, fully fund our savings account, and work towards having our housing expense at 25% of our take home pay. These three steps will take the most time, but will also provide us with the final fuel for a full tank! Once we have completed these three steps, we will have a financial foundation that will allow us to build the lives God has called us to build.

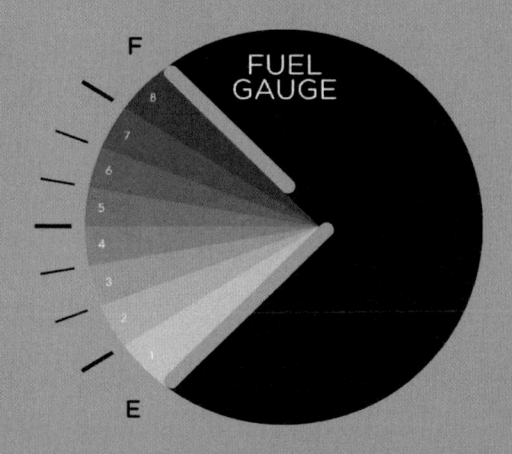

FUEL GAUGE

Stewardship in the Kingdom of God

Session 10
6/8 - Invest 15%, 7/8 - New Zero in Savings, 8/8 - Housing at 25%

Giving Challenge Group Discussion

6/8 - 15% Retirement

Part of laying a healthy foundation is saving _____ of your income for the _____.

_____
_____
_____
_____

If you put _____ of your income away for _____ years, at a conservative _____ average rate of return, you will have enough money in your retirement account to live off of the interest without ever touching the principle.

_____
_____
_____
_____

Answer key

15%
future
15%
25
8%

Stewardship in the Kingdom of God

Session 10
6/8 – Invest 15%, 7/8 – New Zero in Savings, 8/8 – Housing at 25%

If you put _____ of your take home pay into a _____, you'll have a fully _____, tax _____ retirement within _____ years.

Answer key

15%
ROTH 401k
funded
free
25

Breakout Questions

1. Why can saving for retirement be difficult for many people?

2. How has saving for retirement been challenging for you personally?

Stewardship in the Kingdom of God

Session 10

7/8 - New Savings Zero

Just like having a _____ in our checking account for _____, we now need to create a larger _____ for potential _____ of income or other large financial _____.

If your New Checking Zero, which is _____ month of your expenses, is $5,000 then your New Savings Zero is _____.

Your savings account is a _____ of your monthly _____, as that's an indication of your _____. So if you'd like a smaller savings target, that's not a problem! Just _____ _____.

Answer key

- buffer
- emergencies
- buffer
- Loss
- hits
- one
- $25,000
- multiple
- expenses
- lifestyle
- spend less

Stewardship in the Kingdom of God

Session 10
6/8 – Invest 15%, 7/8 – New Zero in Savings, 8/8 – Housing at 25%

8/8 - 25% Housing

Housing Expense includes either your _____ or _____, _____ _____, and _____.

The vast majority of people purchasing a home today have a debt to income ratio of _____-_____.

If you've completed step 8, congratulations!! You have a _____ _____!!! And the _____ and _____ it comes with! Go be all who God created you to be. You have fuel for the journey.

Answer key

mortgage
rent
property taxes
insurance
40-50%
full tank
confidence
freedom

Session 10 // 12   Page 111

Stewardship in the Kingdom of God

Session 10
6/8 - Invest 15%, 7/8 - New Zero in Savings, 8/8 - Housing at 25%

Breakout Questions

1. When your housing expense is 25% of your take home pay, what will that free you to be able to do?

2. What are some limiting beliefs that you're going to have to overcome in order to believe you can hit all three percentages we've discussed? Giving 10%, investing 15% and keeping the housing expense under 25%.

INCREASE

11

Session 11
Build Your Legacy

Everyone leaves a legacy. The task is not to merely leave a legacy, but to build one worth leaving. As we look to the future, we can begin making the appropriate steps today to intentionally leave a legacy that blesses our families and friends, not just with money, but with ethics and wisdom.

Stewardship in the Kingdom of God

> **Session 11**
> Build Your Legacy

Building a Lasting Legacy

We're not pursuing _____, we're pursuing _____. The question is how much _____ do you need to fulfill the _____ of God in your life?

_____
_____
_____
_____

Everyone _____ a _____. The task is not to merely leave a legacy, but to build one _____ _____.

_____
_____
_____
_____

Answer key

intangible
tangible
worth leaving
legacy
leaves
purposes
fuel
purpose
wealth

There will be _____ reminders of your life that you pass on. Things like assets – cash, stocks, real estate, and business interests. And there will be _____ things you leave such as values, morals, and lessons.

_____
_____
_____
_____

Stewardship in the Kingdom of God

> **Session 11**
> Build Your Legacy

Writing your Eulogy

This exercise is a profound journey into self-reflection, focusing on the legacy you wish to leave behind. It's about contemplating the impact of your life from the perspective of those who will remember you.

Eulogy Writing Prompts:

Feel free to write using sentences, paragraphs, bullet points or key words

1. Who Will Be There: Think about the people who will gather to mourn your passing and celebrate your life. Who are they? How have you touched their lives?

2. Words Spoken About You: Imagine what your loved ones, friends, and colleagues would say about you. What words would they use to describe you and your impact on their lives?

Stewardship in the Kingdom of God

Session 11
Build Your Legacy

3. Your Hopes: What do you hope people will remember and say about you? Reflect on the qualities, achievements, or moments you wish to be remembered for.

4. Your Desires: Dive into what you truly want to be said about you. How do you want to be remembered? What legacy do you want to leave in terms of values, contributions, and memories?

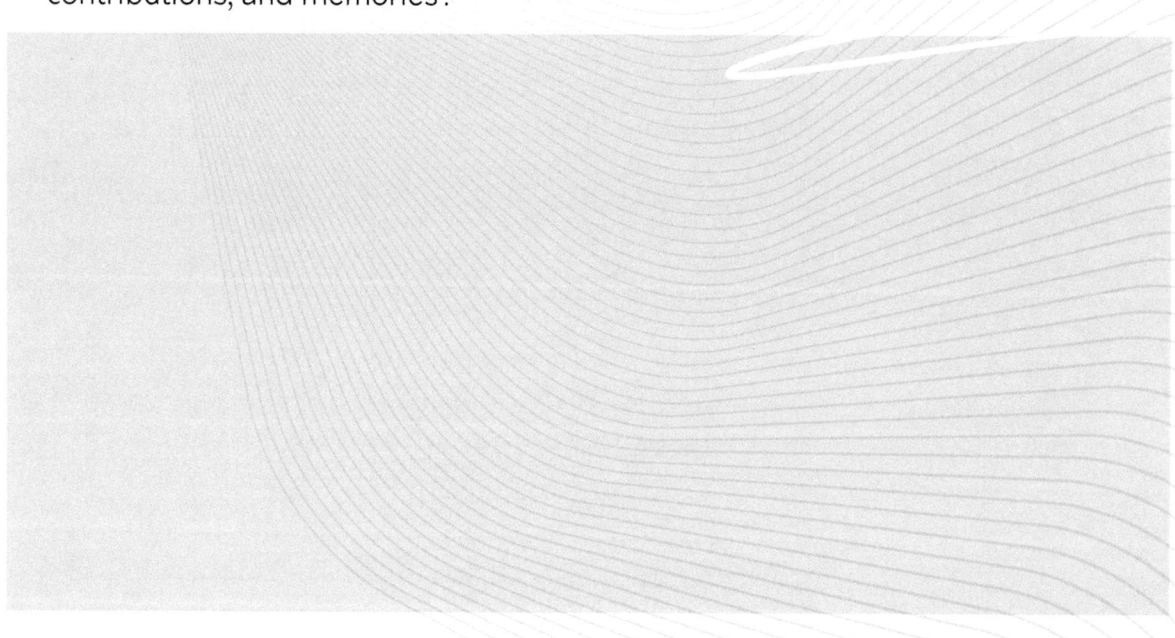

Stewardship in the Kingdom of God

Session 11
Build Your Legacy

Breakout Questions

1. Where did your mind wander as you began to write? What or who did you begin thinking about and why?

2. What do you believe is the most important thing you want to leave behind and why?

Crafting a Legacy: Values, Wills, and Trusts

Just like with purpose and money, legacy planning should start with _____ and END with_____.

Answer key

values
valuables

Session 11 // 12 .   Page 117

Stewardship in the Kingdom of God

Session 11
Build Your Legacy

> "It's better to HAVE a will and not need to use it than to NOT have a will when one is needed."

Your _____ should be reinforced by your _____. Your _____ legacy should be followed by your _____ legacy.

_____
_____
_____
_____

Answer key
values
valuables
intangible
tangible

Stewardship in the Kingdom of God

Session 11
Build Your Legacy

Session 11 Homework

1. Spend time reflecting on your Eulogy. Are you surprised by anything you wrote?

2. What is one action you can take this week to begin living into the legacy you are building?

INCREASE

12
Session 12
Ready, Set, Increase!

You have the information. It's time to put it in place by operating our FUEL Check's effectively month to month. As we do, we must have the right framework for how to live in agreements with ourselves and our spouses. We must also understand that commitment is being willing to move a mountain with a shovel if that is required to do what we said we would do. The ingredients are all here. Will you commit to continuing down the path of Increase?

Stewardship in the Kingdom of God

Session 12
Ready, Set, Increase!

F.U.E.L. Check Guidelines

> "I don't know what God's call is for you, but I do know that we are all part of one Body. If we each pursue God's purposes in our lives without giving up, the world is going to see Christ on display like never before."

The number one thing you can do to produce _____ results in your finances is complete the monthly _____.

_____
_____
_____
_____

The F.U.E.L. Check Worksheet is going to give you a very simple and easy way to check your _____, so please commit to using it for at least the next _____ because it will help keep you on track.

_____
_____
_____
_____

Answer key

consistent
F.U.E.L Check
FUEL
12 months

Stewardship in the Kingdom of God

Session 12
Ready, Set, Increase!

_____ _____ is the thief of _____.

Answer key

Self reliance potential

Breakout Questions

1. What part of the monthly F.U.E.L. Check will be most helpful to you and why?

2. Why is U – Unleashing God's Direction, so important when stewarding our finances?

F.U.E.L. CHECK WORKSHEET

MONTH: _____

F. FINALIZE

	AUDIT Last Month's Spending	+ or - Last Month's Budget	BUDGET This Month
Income			
Take home pay	_____	_____	_____
Take home pay	_____	_____	_____
Total	_____	_____	_____
Expenses			
Retirement	_____	_____	_____
Giving/Generosity	_____	_____	_____
Mortgage/Rent	_____	_____	_____
Car Payment	_____	_____	_____
Other Debt	_____	_____	_____
Insurance	_____	_____	_____
Utilities	_____	_____	_____
Auto/Gas	_____	_____	_____
Groceries	_____	_____	_____
Eating Out	_____	_____	_____
Entertainment	_____	_____	_____
Household Items	_____	_____	_____
Subscriptions	_____	_____	_____
Other _____	_____	_____	_____
Other _____	_____	_____	_____
Other _____	_____	_____	_____
Total	_____	_____	_____
Cash Flow (+/-)	_____	_____	_____

U. UNLEASH GOD'S DIRECTION

E. EVALUATE

FUEL GAUGE (F — 8, 7, 6, 5, 4, 3, 2, 1 — E)

L. LOOK FORWARD

8/8 Housing at 25%
7/8 New Zero in Savings
6/8 Invest 15%
5/8 Consumer Debt Paid Off
4/8 Adequate Insurance
3/8 New Zero in Checking
2/8 Give 10%
1/8 Balanced Budget

Stewardship in the Kingdom of God

Session 12
Ready, Set, Increase!

Seasons

Just like there are 4 seasons in the year, your _____ life also has seasons that vary from month to month. It is okay if some months, you simply _____ your progress.

_____
_____
_____
_____

It is natural and okay for the _____ at which we pursue each target to _____. When major life changes happen, there is a _____ _____ in figuring out your new budget.

_____
_____
_____
_____

There may be _____ when you do go _____. It's not ideal, but it's ok. It's life and sometimes you can't foresee what's up ahead. You've already made forward _____ before, so I know that you can do it _____.

_____
_____
_____
_____

Answer key

financial
maintain
pace
change
learning curve
seasons
backwards
progress
again

Session 12 // 12.   Page 125

Stewardship in the Kingdom of God

> **Session 12**
> Ready, Set, Increase!

> "Discouragement is not of God, it is of the devil. So reject discouragement and shame in your life and remind yourself that you are God's workmanship created to do good works. Throw yourself a little pity party if you need to and then blow the candles out and move on. There's grace in this journey."

Breakout Questions

1. What season are you in right now? Are you in a place where you can put the pedal to the medal or do you need to maintain your progress for a minute? Why?

2. Have you ever failed at a financial system before and been hard on yourself? What would it look like to give yourself or your spouse grace?

Agreements Not Expectations

Because expectations are _____, they cause _____ in their lack of _____.

_____
_____
_____
_____

An agreement is a _____ _____ expectation. There aren't _____ _____ that could potentially provide an out.

_____
_____
_____
_____

To avoid _____ and _____, you must both be on the same page. You shouldn't have fuzzy expectations for one another or for what you're doing, you should have _____ and agree without _____ to your plan moving forward.

_____
_____
_____
_____

Answer key

fuzzy
anxiety
clarity
rock-solid
undefined parameters
bitterness
dissension
clarity
reservation

Stewardship in the Kingdom of God

Session 12
Ready, Set, Increase!

Commitment

An _____ is only as good as the level of _____ behind it.

_____ means moving a _____ with a shovel if that is required to do what I said I would do.

> "Jesus' yoke is easy and his burden is light. His shovel is big and the dirt in your way is as light as the air. Your commitment isn't to work hard in your own strength, but rather, to submit to God's ways and walk in faith, one step at a time down the path He has already prepared in advance for you to walk in."

Answer key

agreement
commitment
Commitment
mountain

Stewardship in the Kingdom of God

Session 12
Ready, Set, Increase!

Breakout Questions

1. What is the difference between expectations and agreements and why is it so important to differentiate and live in agreements?

2. What things do you need to commit to? As you've walked down this path, what has God called you to that you need to commit to pursuing today?

The Path to Increase

As you get ready to launch on the roller coaster of life, I want you to know the instructions _____ and _____.

Answer key

forward
backward

Stewardship in the Kingdom of God

Session 12
Ready, Set, Increase!

As you work through each step on your _____ _____, I want to encourage you to hop back on the ride and listen to the _____.

_____
_____
_____
_____

As you steward your _____ and your _____ Purposes, I am believing that your Specific Purpose will show up and soon, you'll say those beautiful words, "I was _____ for this."

_____
_____
_____
_____
_____

Answer key
F.U.E.L. Gauge
instructions
General
Personal
born

> "Your money has a purpose! It's to fuel God's wonderful purposes in your life. What are you waiting for!? You have the direction and you have the fuel! It's time to live a life of Increase."

INCREASE

F.U.E.L. Check Worksheets

> This is only the beginning. Start right, stay consistent, and be ok with things taking time. All good things have that in common.

F.U.E.L. CHECK WORKSHEET

MONTH: _____

F. FINALIZE

	AUDIT Last Month's Spending	+ or − Last Month's Budget	BUDGET This Month
Income			
Take home pay	_____	_____	_____
Take home pay	_____	_____	_____
Total	_____	_____	_____
Expenses			
Retirement	_____	_____	_____
Giving/Generosity	_____	_____	_____
Mortgage/Rent	_____	_____	_____
Car Payment	_____	_____	_____
Other Debt	_____	_____	_____
Insurance	_____	_____	_____
Utilities	_____	_____	_____
Auto/Gas	_____	_____	_____
Groceries	_____	_____	_____
Eating Out	_____	_____	_____
Entertainment	_____	_____	_____
Household Items	_____	_____	_____
Subscriptions	_____	_____	_____
Other _____	_____	_____	_____
Other _____	_____	_____	_____
Other _____	_____	_____	_____
Total	_____	_____	_____
Cash Flow (+/−)	_____	_____	_____

U. UNLEASH GOD'S DIRECTION

E. EVALUATE

FUEL GAUGE (F — E, 1–8)

L. LOOK FORWARD

8/8 Housing at 25% _____
7/8 New Zero in Savings _____
6/8 Invest 15% _____
5/8 Consumer Debt Paid Off _____
4/8 Adequate Insurance _____
3/8 New Zero in Checking _____
2/8 Give 10% _____
1/8 Balanced Budget _____

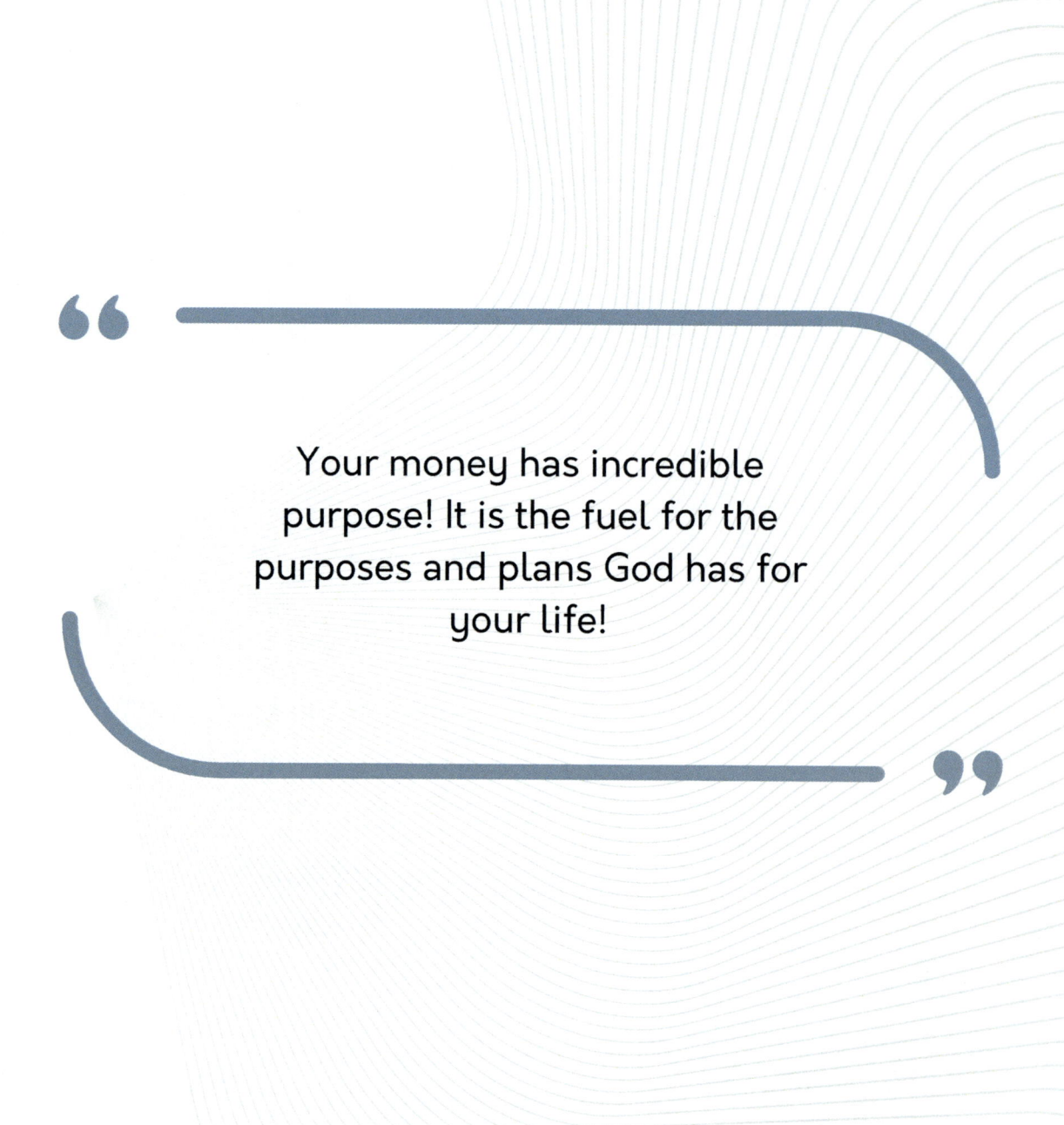

> Your money has incredible purpose! It is the fuel for the purposes and plans God has for your life!

F.U.E.L. CHECK WORKSHEET

MONTH: _____

F. FINALIZE

	AUDIT Last Month's Spending	+ or − Last Month's Budget	BUDGET This Month

Income
- Take home pay
- Take home pay
- **Total**

Expenses
- Retirement
- Giving/Generosity
- Mortgage/Rent
- Car Payment
- Other Debt
- Insurance
- Utilities
- Auto/Gas
- Groceries
- Eating Out
- Entertainment
- Household Items
- Subscriptions
- Other _____
- Other _____
- Other _____
- **Total**

Cash Flow (+/−)

U. UNLEASH GOD'S DIRECTION

E. EVALUATE

FUEL GAUGE (F — 8, 7, 6, 5, 4, 3, 2, 1 — E)

L. LOOK FORWARD

- 8/8 Housing at 25%
- 7/8 New Zero in Savings
- 6/8 Invest 15%
- 5/8 Consumer Debt Paid Off
- 4/8 Adequate Insurance
- 3/8 New Zero in Checking
- 2/8 Give 10%
- 1/8 Balanced Budget

> Giving away your first 10% aligns your heart with God's so you can properly steward the remaining 90% of your budget each month.

F.U.E.L. CHECK WORKSHEET

MONTH: _____

F. FINALIZE

	AUDIT Last Month's Spending	+ or − Last Month's Budget	BUDGET This Month
Income			
Take home pay	_____	_____	_____
Take home pay	_____	_____	_____
Total	_____	_____	_____
Expenses			
Retirement	_____	_____	_____
Giving/Generosity	_____	_____	_____
Mortgage/Rent	_____	_____	_____
Car Payment	_____	_____	_____
Other Debt	_____	_____	_____
Insurance	_____	_____	_____
Utilities	_____	_____	_____
Auto/Gas	_____	_____	_____
Groceries	_____	_____	_____
Eating Out	_____	_____	_____
Entertainment	_____	_____	_____
Household Items	_____	_____	_____
Subscriptions	_____	_____	_____
Other _____	_____	_____	_____
Other _____	_____	_____	_____
Other _____	_____	_____	_____
Total	_____	_____	_____
Cash Flow (+/−)	_____	_____	_____

U. UNLEASH GOD'S DIRECTION

E. EVALUATE

FUEL GAUGE (F — E, 1–8)

L. LOOK FORWARD

- 8/8 Housing at 25%
- 7/8 New Zero in Savings
- 6/8 Invest 15%
- 5/8 Consumer Debt Paid Off
- 4/8 Adequate Insurance
- 3/8 New Zero in Checking
- 2/8 Give 10%
- 1/8 Balanced Budget

> There is grace in this journey. Remember the principle of seasons. It's ok to sometimes maintain your progress for one or two months.

F.U.E.L. CHECK WORKSHEET

MONTH: _____

F. FINALIZE

	AUDIT Last Month's Spending	+ or – Last Month's Budget	BUDGET This Month
Income			
Take home pay	_____	_____	_____
Take home pay	_____	_____	_____
Total	_____	_____	_____
Expenses			
Retirement	_____	_____	_____
Giving/Generosity	_____	_____	_____
Mortgage/Rent	_____	_____	_____
Car Payment	_____	_____	_____
Other Debt	_____	_____	_____
Insurance	_____	_____	_____
Utilities	_____	_____	_____
Auto/Gas	_____	_____	_____
Groceries	_____	_____	_____
Eating Out	_____	_____	_____
Entertainment	_____	_____	_____
Household Items	_____	_____	_____
Subscriptions	_____	_____	_____
Other _____	_____	_____	_____
Other _____	_____	_____	_____
Other _____	_____	_____	_____
Total	_____	_____	_____
Cash Flow (+/–)	_____	_____	_____

U. UNLEASH GOD'S DIRECTION

E. EVALUATE

FUEL GAUGE (F to E, 1–8)

L. LOOK FORWARD

8/8 **Housing at 25%**

7/8 **New Zero in Savings**

6/8 **Invest 15%**

5/8 **Consumer Debt Paid Off**

4/8 **Adequate Insurance**

3/8 **New Zero in Checking**

2/8 **Give 10%**

1/8 **Balanced Budget**

> "You're going to have a hard time making forward progress if you don't address your income. Increasing your income is the fastest way to a full tank!"

F.U.E.L. CHECK WORKSHEET

MONTH: _____

F. FINALIZE

	AUDIT Last Month's Spending	+ or - Last Month's Budget	BUDGET This Month
Income			
Take home pay	_____	_____	_____
Take home pay	_____	_____	_____
Total	_____	_____	_____
Expenses			
Retirement	_____	_____	_____
Giving/Generosity	_____	_____	_____
Mortgage/Rent	_____	_____	_____
Car Payment	_____	_____	_____
Other Debt	_____	_____	_____
Insurance	_____	_____	_____
Utilities	_____	_____	_____
Auto/Gas	_____	_____	_____
Groceries	_____	_____	_____
Eating Out	_____	_____	_____
Entertainment	_____	_____	_____
Household Items	_____	_____	_____
Subscriptions	_____	_____	_____
Other _____	_____	_____	_____
Other _____	_____	_____	_____
Other _____	_____	_____	_____
Total	_____	_____	_____
Cash Flow (+/-)	_____	_____	_____

U. UNLEASH GOD'S DIRECTION

E. EVALUATE

FUEL GAUGE (F to E, 1–8)

L. LOOK FORWARD

8/8 Housing at 25%

7/8 New Zero in Savings

6/8 Invest 15%

5/8 Consumer Debt Paid Off

4/8 Adequate Insurance

3/8 New Zero in Checking

2/8 Give 10%

1/8 Balanced Budget

> You are God's handiwork. Don't forget that your life has a purpose. It isn't just about money. Money is only the fuel for your G.P.S.!

F.U.E.L. CHECK WORKSHEET

MONTH: _____

F. FINALIZE

	AUDIT Last Month's Spending	+ or - Last Month's Budget	BUDGET This Month
Income			
Take home pay	_____	_____	_____
Take home pay	_____	_____	_____
Total	_____	_____	_____
Expenses			
Retirement	_____	_____	_____
Giving/Generosity	_____	_____	_____
Mortgage/Rent	_____	_____	_____
Car Payment	_____	_____	_____
Other Debt	_____	_____	_____
Insurance	_____	_____	_____
Utilities	_____	_____	_____
Auto/Gas	_____	_____	_____
Groceries	_____	_____	_____
Eating Out	_____	_____	_____
Entertainment	_____	_____	_____
Household Items	_____	_____	_____
Subscriptions	_____	_____	_____
Other _____	_____	_____	_____
Other _____	_____	_____	_____
Other _____	_____	_____	_____
Total	_____	_____	_____
Cash Flow (+/-)	_____	_____	_____

U. UNLEASH GOD'S DIRECTION

E. EVALUATE

FUEL GAUGE

L. LOOK FORWARD

8/8 Housing at 25%

7/8 New Zero in Savings

6/8 Invest 15%

5/8 Consumer Debt Paid Off

4/8 Adequate Insurance

3/8 New Zero in Checking

2/8 Give 10%

1/8 Balanced Budget

> Your value has a price tag. What value are you bringing to the marketplace and how can you meaningfully increase that value this month?

F.U.E.L. CHECK WORKSHEET

MONTH: _____

F. FINALIZE

	AUDIT Last Month's Spending	+ or – Last Month's Budget	BUDGET This Month
Income			
Take home pay	---------	---------	---------
Take home pay	---------	---------	---------
Total	---------	---------	---------
Expenses			
Retirement	---------	---------	---------
Giving/Generosity	---------	---------	---------
Mortgage/Rent	---------	---------	---------
Car Payment	---------	---------	---------
Other Debt	---------	---------	---------
Insurance	---------	---------	---------
Utilities	---------	---------	---------
Auto/Gas	---------	---------	---------
Groceries	---------	---------	---------
Eating Out	---------	---------	---------
Entertainment	---------	---------	---------
Household Items	---------	---------	---------
Subscriptions	---------	---------	---------
Other _____	---------	---------	---------
Other _____	---------	---------	---------
Other _____	---------	---------	---------
Total	---------	---------	---------
Cash Flow (+/-)	---------	---------	---------

U. UNLEASH GOD'S DIRECTION

E. EVALUATE

FUEL GAUGE (F — E, 1–8)

L. LOOK FORWARD

8/8 **Housing at 25%** _____
7/8 **New Zero in Savings** _____
6/8 **Invest 15%** _____
5/8 **Consumer Debt Paid Off** _____
4/8 **Adequate Insurance** _____
3/8 **New Zero in Checking** _____
2/8 **Give 10%** _____
1/8 **Balanced Budget** _____

> Who are you becoming on this journey? Whether you realize it or not, you are actively building a legacy. Is it one worth leaving?

F.U.E.L. CHECK WORKSHEET

MONTH: _____

F. FINALIZE

	AUDIT Last Month's Spending	+ or - Last Month's Budget	BUDGET This Month
Income			
Take home pay	_____	_____	_____
Take home pay	_____	_____	_____
Total	_____	_____	_____
Expenses			
Retirement	_____	_____	_____
Giving/Generosity	_____	_____	_____
Mortgage/Rent	_____	_____	_____
Car Payment	_____	_____	_____
Other Debt	_____	_____	_____
Insurance	_____	_____	_____
Utilities	_____	_____	_____
Auto/Gas	_____	_____	_____
Groceries	_____	_____	_____
Eating Out	_____	_____	_____
Entertainment	_____	_____	_____
Household Items	_____	_____	_____
Subscriptions	_____	_____	_____
Other _____	_____	_____	_____
Other _____	_____	_____	_____
Other _____	_____	_____	_____
Total	_____	_____	_____
Cash Flow (+/-)	_____	_____	_____

U. UNLEASH GOD'S DIRECTION

E. EVALUATE

FUEL GAUGE (F to E, 1–8)

L. LOOK FORWARD

8/8 Housing at 25%

7/8 New Zero in Savings

6/8 Invest 15%

5/8 Consumer Debt Paid Off

4/8 Adequate Insurance

3/8 New Zero in Checking

2/8 Give 10%

1/8 Balanced Budget

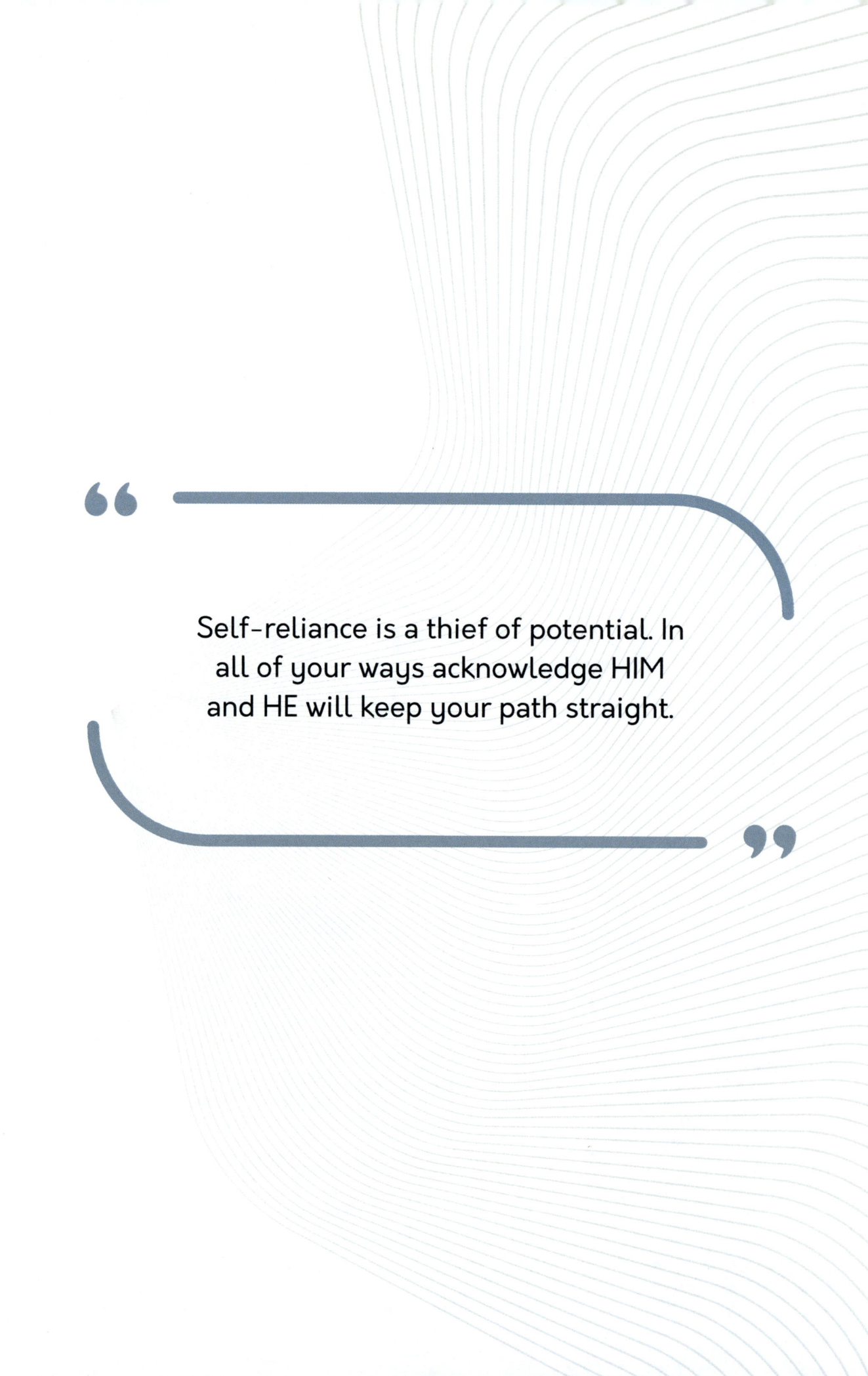

> Self-reliance is a thief of potential. In all of your ways acknowledge HIM and HE will keep your path straight.

F.U.E.L. CHECK WORKSHEET

MONTH: _____

F. FINALIZE

	AUDIT Last Month's Spending	+ or − Last Month's Budget	BUDGET This Month
Income			
Take home pay	_____	_____	_____
Take home pay	_____	_____	_____
Total	_____	_____	_____
Expenses			
Retirement	_____	_____	_____
Giving/Generosity	_____	_____	_____
Mortgage/Rent	_____	_____	_____
Car Payment	_____	_____	_____
Other Debt	_____	_____	_____
Insurance	_____	_____	_____
Utilities	_____	_____	_____
Auto/Gas	_____	_____	_____
Groceries	_____	_____	_____
Eating Out	_____	_____	_____
Entertainment	_____	_____	_____
Household Items	_____	_____	_____
Subscriptions	_____	_____	_____
Other _____	_____	_____	_____
Other _____	_____	_____	_____
Other _____	_____	_____	_____
Total	_____	_____	_____
Cash Flow (+/−)	_____	_____	_____

U. UNLEASH GOD'S DIRECTION

E. EVALUATE

FUEL GAUGE (F — 8,7,6,5,4,3,2,1 — E)

L. LOOK FORWARD

8/8 Housing at 25%
7/8 New Zero in Savings
6/8 Invest 15%
5/8 Consumer Debt Paid Off
4/8 Adequate Insurance
3/8 New Zero in Checking
2/8 Give 10%
1/8 Balanced Budget

> Keep your head in the clouds and your feet on the ground. Look forward, but have a plan and execute that plan to the best of your ability.

F.U.E.L. CHECK WORKSHEET

MONTH: _____

F. FINALIZE

	AUDIT Last Month's Spending	+ or − Last Month's Budget	BUDGET This Month
Income			
Take home pay	_____	_____	_____
Take home pay	_____	_____	_____
Total	_____	_____	_____
Expenses			
Retirement	_____	_____	_____
Giving/Generosity	_____	_____	_____
Mortgage/Rent	_____	_____	_____
Car Payment	_____	_____	_____
Other Debt	_____	_____	_____
Insurance	_____	_____	_____
Utilities	_____	_____	_____
Auto/Gas	_____	_____	_____
Groceries	_____	_____	_____
Eating Out	_____	_____	_____
Entertainment	_____	_____	_____
Household Items	_____	_____	_____
Subscriptions	_____	_____	_____
Other _____	_____	_____	_____
Other _____	_____	_____	_____
Other _____	_____	_____	_____
Total	_____	_____	_____
Cash Flow (+/−)	_____	_____	_____

U. UNLEASH GOD'S DIRECTION

E. EVALUATE

FUEL GAUGE (F to E)

L. LOOK FORWARD

8/8 Housing at 25%

7/8 New Zero in Savings

6/8 Invest 15%

5/8 Consumer Debt Paid Off

4/8 Adequate Insurance

3/8 New Zero in Checking

2/8 Give 10%

1/8 Balanced Budget

> Be so committed that you would move a mountain with a shovel if that is required to do what you said you would do!

F.U.E.L. CHECK WORKSHEET

MONTH: _____

F. FINALIZE

	AUDIT Last Month's Spending	+ or − Last Month's Budget	BUDGET This Month
Income			
Take home pay	_____	_____	_____
Take home pay	_____	_____	_____
Total	_____	_____	_____
Expenses			
Retirement	_____	_____	_____
Giving/Generosity	_____	_____	_____
Mortgage/Rent	_____	_____	_____
Car Payment	_____	_____	_____
Other Debt	_____	_____	_____
Insurance	_____	_____	_____
Utilities	_____	_____	_____
Auto/Gas	_____	_____	_____
Groceries	_____	_____	_____
Eating Out	_____	_____	_____
Entertainment	_____	_____	_____
Household Items	_____	_____	_____
Subscriptions	_____	_____	_____
Other _____	_____	_____	_____
Other _____	_____	_____	_____
Other _____	_____	_____	_____
Total	_____	_____	_____
Cash Flow (+/−)	_____	_____	_____

U. UNLEASH GOD'S DIRECTION

E. EVALUATE

FUEL GAUGE (F — E)

L. LOOK FORWARD

8/8 Housing at 25%

7/8 New Zero in Savings

6/8 Invest 15%

5/8 Consumer Debt Paid Off

4/8 Adequate Insurance

3/8 New Zero in Checking

2/8 Give 10%

1/8 Balanced Budget

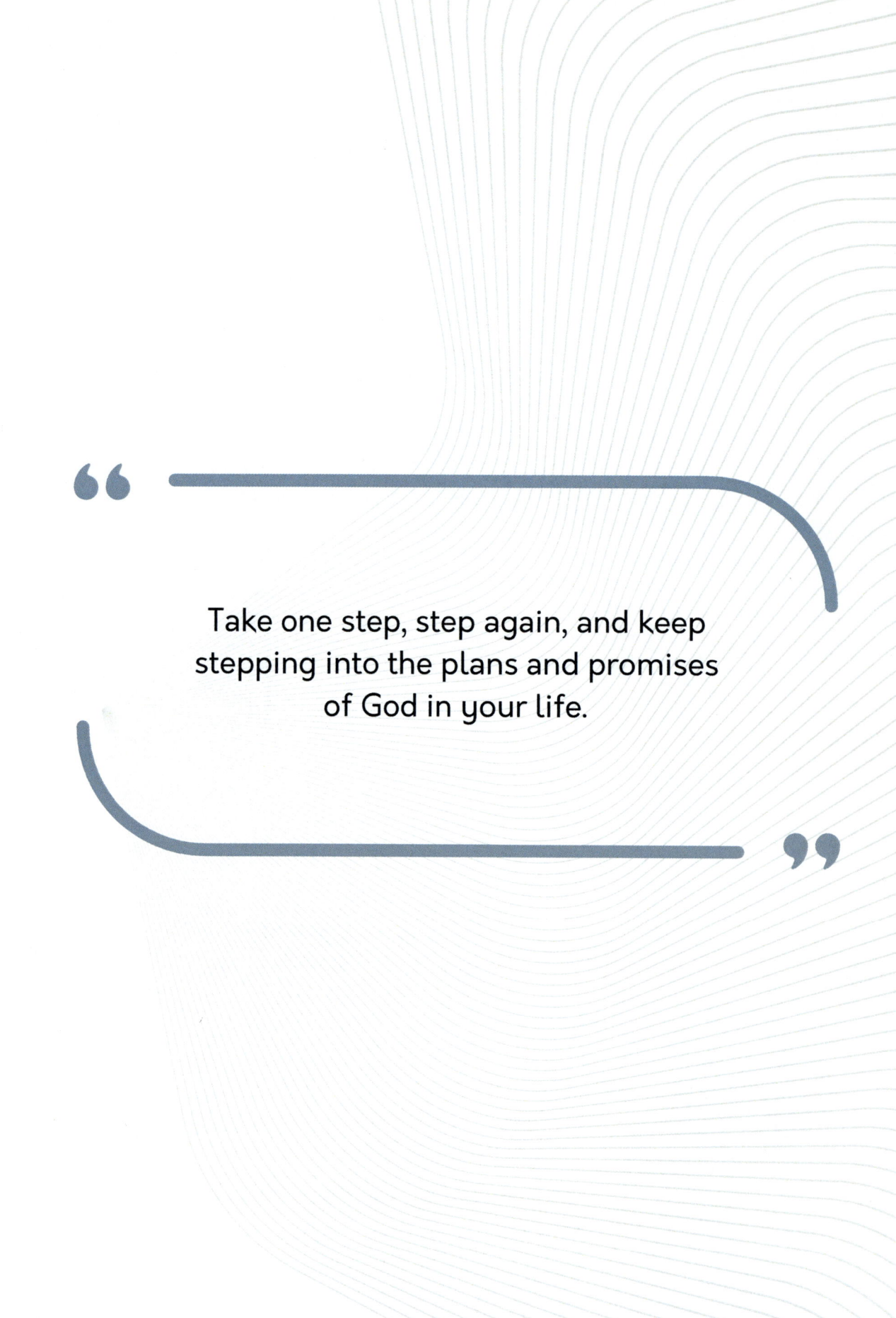

> Take one step, step again, and keep stepping into the plans and promises of God in your life.

F.U.E.L. CHECK WORKSHEET

MONTH: _____

F. FINALIZE

	AUDIT Last Month's Spending	+ or − Last Month's Budget	BUDGET This Month
Income			
Take home pay	_____	_____	_____
Take home pay	_____	_____	_____
Total	_____	_____	_____
Expenses			
Retirement	_____	_____	_____
Giving/Generosity	_____	_____	_____
Mortgage/Rent	_____	_____	_____
Car Payment	_____	_____	_____
Other Debt	_____	_____	_____
Insurance	_____	_____	_____
Utilities	_____	_____	_____
Auto/Gas	_____	_____	_____
Groceries	_____	_____	_____
Eating Out	_____	_____	_____
Entertainment	_____	_____	_____
Household Items	_____	_____	_____
Subscriptions	_____	_____	_____
Other _____	_____	_____	_____
Other _____	_____	_____	_____
Other _____	_____	_____	_____
Total	_____	_____	_____
Cash Flow (+/−)	_____	_____	_____

U. UNLEASH GOD'S DIRECTION

E. EVALUATE

FUEL GAUGE
F
8
7
6
5
4
3
2
1
E

L. LOOK FORWARD

8/8 Housing at 25% _____
7/8 New Zero in Savings _____
6/8 Invest 15% _____
5/8 Consumer Debt Paid Off _____
4/8 Adequate Insurance _____
3/8 New Zero in Checking _____
2/8 Give 10% _____
1/8 Balanced Budget _____

> Welcome to the beginning of your "full tank" life!

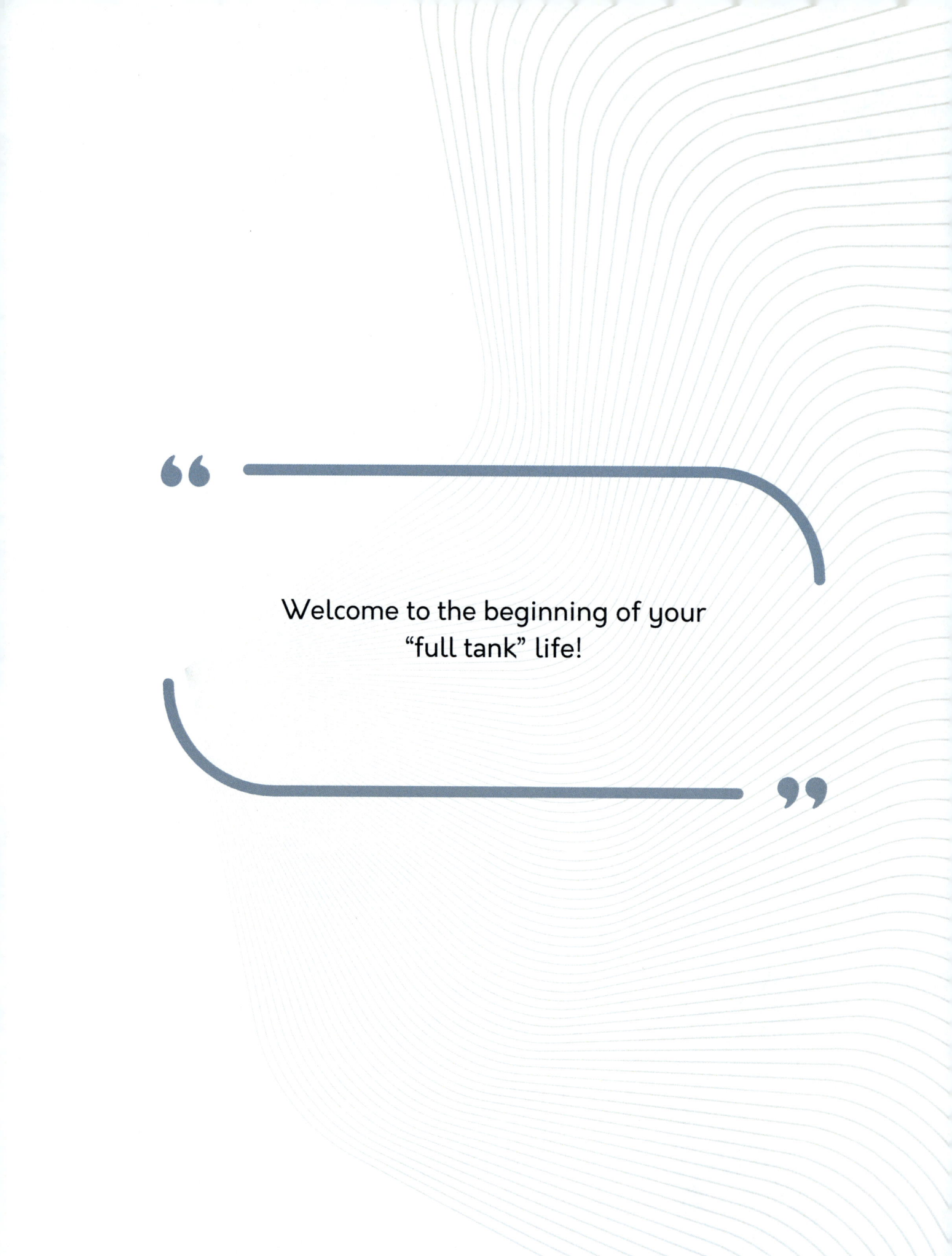

Made in the USA
Columbia, SC
03 February 2024

831dea9a-7ab4-4d08-aae1-4c8a7ff1f015R01